원서 술술 읽는
Smart
Reading 1

원서 술술 읽는 Smart Reading 1

지은이 넥서스영어교육연구소
펴낸이 임상진
펴낸곳 (주)넥서스

출판신고 1992년 4월 3일 제311-2002-2호 ②
10880 경기도 파주시 지목로 5
Tel (02)330-5500 Fax (02)330-5555

ISBN 979-11-5752-510-2   54740
      979-11-5752-509-6 (SET)

www.nexusEDU.kr
NEXUS Edu는 넥서스의 초·중·고 학습물 전문 브랜드입니다.

원서 술술 읽는
Smart Reading

넥서스영어교육연구소 지음

1

NEXUS Edu

Introduction

Dear Students,

Language learning is a part of your journey to academic success. It can open up many doors and provide you with many opportunities for your future. All four skills (reading, writing, listening and speaking) are important, but reading may be the skill that is most critical to your success in both general language learning as well as test-taking. You are certainly going to face more tests as you continue in school, and reading is the key to doing well on those tests. Indeed, research has shown that reading has the greatest effect on overall language learning success and is the most important factor in getting high TOEFL scores.

Smart Reading is composed of high-interest passages that explore unusual, fascinating topics to spark your imagination. At the same time it focuses on the language you will need for academic success and the language you will use as your language learning journey continues.

Smart Reading is designed to increase your enjoyment of reading, improve your grammar skills, increase your vocabulary and help you comprehend what you read more effectively and efficiently. For each passage there is a pre-reading activity that will give you some interesting facts about the topic and prepare your mind to process the information in the passage. The questions after each passage and the review exercises at the end of each unit will enable you to begin to master the types of questions you will encounter in tests like the foreign language high school exam, the TOEFL test, and the Korean SAT.

We hope you enjoy the passages in this book and we hope the varied and extensive exercises will help you achieve success in English and in your academic future.

Composition of the Book

Reading Passages:

Each book is composed of 32 passages which give students knowledge of various and useful topics. Vocabulary and English structures in each passage are designed to help students not only improve their reading skills but also foster their logical thinking skills.

Pre-reading Activity:

Pre-reading Activity gives students some interesting facts about the topic and hints on what the passage is about.

Reading Tips:

Reading Tips are designed to give students useful expressions or additional interesting information. Through the Reading Tips, students get the opportunity to study useful idioms, phrasal verbs, and grammar.

Comprehension Questions:

Comprehension Questions of various types are designed to help students prepare for the Korean SAT, TOEFL, and foreign language high school exams. Students can check how well they understand each passage and they can also master the types of questions they will encounter on these exams.

Unit Review:

Students have a chance to review the words and the expressions that they have been exposed to in the passages. They can also practice grammar that is crucial to enhancing reading skills.

Table of Contents

▶ ▶

Table of Contents

정답 및 해설

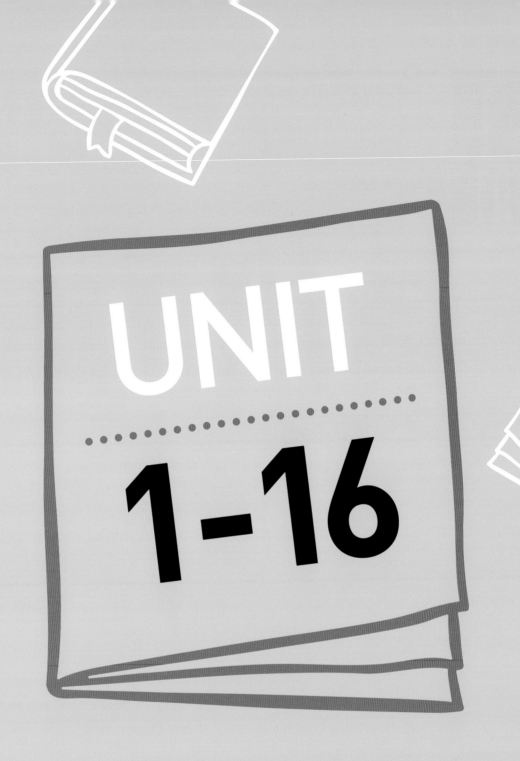

UNIT

1-16

THE NEW WORLD ECONOMY

Economic Rise of China

Pre-reading Activity

Look at the title of the passage. Circle the words you think will be in the passage:

communist	construction	Beijing	subway
automobiles	skyscrapers	Shanghai	bicycle

Now scan the passage and see if you were right. How many? _____

China's economy has grown quickly since the late 1970s. Before then, China   1
had a strictly communist style of government. However, approximately 53% of
the population was in poverty, and China had very little trade with the rest of the
world. Since the market reforms of 1979, the standard of living has improved.
The economy has become larger and more complex every year. Depending on the   5
measure used, it is either the second or third largest in the world. Despite China's
amazing achievements, there are still many challenges.

Consumer safety is a big problem in China. Because so many businesses
have sprung up, creating so much competition, every business owner wants to
get ahead. There are few government safety regulations, and they are difficult to   10
enforce. For these reasons, some businesses have cut costs in dangerous ways by
adding melamine to dairy products, harmful chemicals to children's medicine,
and so on. As a result, many people in other countries are concerned about food
and medicine sourced from China.

Environmental pollution is another well-known issue. It is another result of   15
the government's lax regulation. Much of China's electricity comes from coal,
which produces a great deal of soot. Because of smoke from coal-burning power
plants, exhaust from the millions of cars Chinese people can now afford, and
factory emissions, the air over cities like Beijing, Guangzhou, and Xian is often
brown.   20

The government of China knows it is facing serious problems, and it
is acting to resolve them. For example, there is a new safety organization
to regulate food and medicine. The government is looking into new sources
of electricity. Major cities are building subway systems to cut down on
automobile use. China will continue to be a   25
prosperous nation for a long time if these
challenges can be met.

Reading Tips

forms of government

Communism is a system in which the government controls the production of all food and goods, and there is no privately owned property.

Monarchy is a system in which a country is ruled by a king or queen.

Democracy is a system in which every citizen in the country can vote to elect its government officials.

A federal system is one where individual states control their own affairs, but a national government is responsible for areas such as defense and foreign policy.

1   What is the main idea of the passage?

    a. a strict foreign policy in China

    b. China's history since the 20th century

    c. a big change in China's political system

    d. effect of economic development on China

    e. China's problem with environmental pollution

2   Which is closest in meaning to the word "prosperous"?

    a. vicious

    b. thriving

    c. harmful

    d. prospective

    e. humongous

3   What can be inferred from the passage?

    a. Medicine from China may be unsafe.

    b. Chinese eggs are full of harmful bacteria.

    c. Insects are often found in bags of frozen vegetables.

    d. Chinese chairs break and kill people who sit in them.

    e. Cardboard can be found inside traditional meat dumplings.

4   Why is consumer safety such a problem in China?

    a. Many workers are careless.

    b. Quality is not important in China.

    c. Safety equipment is too expensive.

    d. Safety regulations are not enforced.

    e. It keeps the population from increasing.

5   What are some problems in China resulting from its economic rise?

_____

A Win-Win Situation

Pre-reading Activity

Would you like to run your own business? If yes, what kind of business?

How do you think businesses should help their customers or their communities? Circle the ideas you like.

support local schools   donate some profits   reduce prices

support the homeless   provide loans to employees

A common stereotype of businesspeople is that they are heartless capitalists who are only out to make a buck, no matter what it takes. However, there is a new business leadership role, the social entrepreneur. He or she is seeking to make the world a better place, while also earning a profit.

Worldwide, one in four people lives without electricity. They have to use ⁵ kerosene lanterns after the sun goes down. However, kerosene is expensive, causes pollution, and creates dangerous fumes. One social entrepreneur wants to replace the world's kerosene lanterns with solar-powered LED lamps and flashlights. These lights feature batteries that charge during the day and then can be used at night. These are more cost-effective than the kerosene alternative, and ¹⁰ they are also much cleaner and healthier. His company makes a profit selling them, and his customers save money by using them. It's a win-win situation.

Perhaps the world's most famous social entrepreneur is Muhammad Yunus. The winner of the 2006 Nobel Peace Prize, Yunus is the founder of Grameen Bank in Bangladesh and a pioneer in the field of microfinance. Microfinance is ¹⁵ the process by which poor individuals are able to borrow small sums of money to start new businesses or expand existing ones. Yunus wanted to help his country's people by showing them how to help themselves. He did this by providing loans on suitable terms and teaching them sound financial principles. It's hard for the poor to get loans from traditional banks. Microfinance seemed like a bad idea at ²⁰ first because of high repayment risks. Now that the trend has caught on, though, people in lower-income areas have access to new business opportunities.

While all businesses exist to make a profit, some entrepreneurs have proven that the ideas of profit and doing good don't have to be mutually exclusive. ²⁵

Reading Tips

Bangladesh is a country in South Asia. It is bordered by India on all sides except for a small border with Myanmar to the southeast and by the Bay of Bengal to the south. The capital of Bangladesh is Dhaka. Bengali is the official language.

1 **What is the best alternative title of the passage?**

a. Doing Good and Making a Profit
b. Environmentally-friendly Businesses
c. Great Businessmen from Bangladesh
d. A Social Entrepreneur: Muhammad Yunus
e. Development Schemes for Poor Countries

2 **What is a common, if not always true, belief about businesspeople?**

a. Money is not important to them.
b. They are only interested in money.
c. Most of them did not do well in school.
d. They spend a lot of money on education.
e. They care very much about other people.

3 **What does the word "them" refer to?**

a. loans
b. suitable terms
c. financial principles
d. some entrepreneurs
e. poor Bangladeshis

4 **Why does the author mention "mutually exclusive"?**

a. to imply that microfinance is a very risky venture
b. to suggest that microfinance is unlikely to succeed
c. to say that it is wrong to earn money from helping people
d. to show that it is possible to help people while earning a profit
e. to imply that many people want help through microfinance loans

5 **What does a social entrepreneur do?**

A Words

A1. Fill in the blank according to the definition.

heartless	prosperous	lax	harmful	access

1 _____: having financial success

2 _____: doing something in a careless or lazy way

3 _____: the right to enter a place or to use something

4 _____: without feeling normal human feelings such as sympathy, humor

5 _____: injuring, damaging, or having a bad effect on someone or something

A2. Choose the most appropriate word for each blank.

1 The labor unions held a meeting to _____ the conflict.
   a. learn   b. resolve   c. ask   d. think

2 All the _____ from the auction will be contributed to charity.
   a. taxes   b. loss   c. profits   d. loans

3 My computer died, so it needed to be _____ as soon as possible.
   a. replaced   b. refreshed   c. released   d. rearranged

4 The government announced that new regulations on imports would be _____ enforced.
   a. lately   b. unusually   c. strictly   d. quietly

5 To keep people safe, the government has established tough _____ for drug companies.
   a. chemicals   b. definitions   c. inspectors   d. standards

A3. Complete each sentence with one of the words from the box.

soot	poverty	stereotype	founder	alternative

1 I hate flying; as a(n) _____, I like to take the train.

2 _____ is a problem no one has found a way to solve.

3 It is a(n) _____ that all Asian students are good at science and math.

4 The buildings in Budapest are covered with _____ because of pollution.

5 Bill Gates, the _____ of Microsoft, built Bill & Melinda Gates Foundation.

B Expressions and Phrases

B1. Fill in the blank using an expression from the box.

as a result	no matter what	in the field of	mutually exclusive

1 Happiness and sadness are not _____.

2 He lied to his boss, got caught, and was fired _____.

3 Today's guest speaker is a leader _____ urban planning.

4 _____, your grades are the most important thing. Don't fail the class!

B2. Complete each sentence with an expression from the reading passages.
(Change the form of the verb if necessary.)

get ahead	spring up	look into	make a buck

1 It's not easy to _____ during such difficult economic times.

2 Convenience stores have rapidly _____ all over the country.

3 If you want to _____ in politics, you have to look confident.

4 Someone broke into my apartment yesterday, so now the police _____ it.

C Summary

Complete the summary with the appropriate words and expressions.

borrow	entrepreneurs	poverty	social
unprecedented	enacted	potential	develop

Until 1979, when the market reforms were _____, China's economy was not large, and many people lived in _____. After that, China's growth has been _____. Though problems like consumer safety and poor government oversight persist, China still has great _____ for continued growth.

Social _____ are business owners who are interested in both profit and positive social change. They may _____ and sell environmentally-friendly products, for example. Microfinance, which enables poor people in developing countries to _____ money for businesses, is an excellent example of _____ entrepreneurship.

GREAT WORLD LEADERS

Mohandas Gandhi

Pre-reading Activity

Fill in the blanks using the words *influential*, *movement*, and *non-violent*.

Mohandas Gandhi was the leader of the Indian nationalist _____ against the British rule. His philosophy of _____ protest to achieve political and social progress is hugely _____ even now.

Gandhi is well-known all over the world today as the father of modern 1
India. He successfully fought for India's independence from Great Britain using a campaign of non-violent civil disobedience. He is often called Mahatma, meaning the Great Soul.

Born in 1869 in India, Gandhi went to London for university to study law 5
when he was nineteen years old. In 1893, he traveled to South Africa. The trip to South Africa was a turning point in his life. Indians in South Africa were the victims of many xenophobic laws, and this <u>outraged</u> Gandhi. He organized non-violent protests to fight against the laws, encouraging Indians to burn their identity cards and not to cooperate with authorities. Gandhi was jailed more than 10
once for this type of civil disobedience.

In 1915, Gandhi returned to India. Immediately upon his return, he began organizing protests to oppose the oppressive and unjust British rule. Later, after a horrible massacre of Indians by the British, Gandhi began to call for India's independence. Gandhi told Indians not to buy British products or work in 15
government jobs and to ignore all British law. In 1922, he was imprisoned, even though his protests were always non-violent.

In 1930, Gandhi and seventy-eight followers marched 400 kilometers to the ocean to make their own salt. This act was illegal because under the law all salt had to be bought from the British government. In response to this demonstration, 20
the British government incarcerated 60,000 Indians. However, by this time, the British were finding it very difficult to govern India. The citizens, led by Gandhi, refused to pay taxes, work, or do anything related to helping the government.
In 1947, the British found India to be ungovernable and relinquished control of the country to an Indian government headed by Gandhi. Unfortunately, the Great Soul was assassinated a year later.

25

Reading Tips

verbs that take infinitives as objects: agree, ask, choose, decide, expect, hope, pretend, promise, refuse, seem, want, etc.
I want to tell you something.

verbs that take gerunds as objects: admit, avoid, consider, delay, deny, enjoy, finish, give up, mind, postpone, suggest, etc.
I finished painting my house just minutes ago.

1 **What is the main idea of the passage?**

a. Mohandas Gandhi's trip to South Africa

b. Indians' struggling under the British rule

c. why Mohandas Gandhi was assassinated

d. life and achievements of Mohandas Gandhi

e. reasons Mohandas Gandhi returned to India

2 **Which is closest in meaning to the word "outraged"?**

a. pleased

b. angered

c. depressed

d. understood

e. cheered up

3 **Which of the following is true?**

a. Mohandas Gandhi was born and grew up in London.

b. Mohandas Gandhi urged Indians to destroy their identity cards.

c. Mohandas Gandhi spied on the British government for his country.

d. Gandhi was expelled from his country because of his disobedience.

e. After Gandhi's assassination, India gained independence from the British.

4 **What event directly made Gandhi decide India should be independent?**

a. There was a civil war in India.

b. Many Indian people were killed by the British.

c. Other neighboring countries became independent.

d. Indians suffered from many xenophobic laws in South Africa.

e. The British government imprisoned Gandhi for his disobedience.

5 **What was the reason Indians could not make their own salt?**

Abraham Lincoln

Pre-reading Activity

1. Which of the following American presidents were assassinated while serving as president?

Abraham Lincoln	Warren G. Harding	John F. Kennedy
Ronald Reagan	James A. Garfield	William McKinley

2. How long is a term of office for a US president?

_____

Abraham Lincoln is one of the most famous American presidents because he deftly guided the United States through a difficult time. (A) , many consider it one of the darkest periods in the history of this young country. Lincoln is known for leading the Union (the northern states) to victory during his country's civil war and for setting the slaves free. 5

Born to undistinguished parents in 1809, Lincoln grew up on a farm in Kentucky. Before becoming president he held several jobs. He was a captain in the Black Hawk War; he practiced law; and he served in the Illinois state legislature for eight years. He somehow found the time to marry Mary Todd, (B) gave him four children. 10

In 1858, Lincoln ran against Stephen A. Douglas for a senate seat from the state of Illinois and lost! But in debating with Douglas he gained a wide, national following that later helped him to win the presidency in 1860. As president, he built his party into a strong national organization and forged a coalition with other groups to oppose the Confederacy (the southern states) and their slave- 15 based economy.

From 1861 to 1865, the U.S. Civil War threatened to rip apart the country, but Lincoln's steady leadership won victory. During the war, on January 1, 1863, he delivered the famous Emancipation Proclamation that forever freed the slaves within the southern states. He was later re-elected president in 1864. 20

Lincoln was a great president in both war and peace. In his planning for the peace, Abraham Lincoln was flexible and generous, encouraging Southerners to lay down their weapons and once again join the United States. His policies helped to heal a divided country. He did not live long after the war. On April 14, 1865, he was 25 assassinated at Ford's Theater in Washington, D.C. by John Wilkes Booth.

Reading Tips

The Emancipation Proclamation is an announcement made in the U.S. by President Abraham Lincoln during the American Civil War. He ordered the end of slavery (the practice of owning people as property) in the Confederate States (the southern states of the U.S.) from January 1, 1863. Soon after the war, slavery was completely ended by the "13th Amendment" to the U.S. Constitution.

1 **What is the passage mainly about?**

a. Abraham Lincoln's political partners
b. Abraham Lincoln's assassination
c. Abraham Lincoln's presidency
d. Abraham Lincoln's childhood
e. Abraham Lincoln's life

2 **Which is closest in meaning to the word "delivered"?**

a. wrote
b. brought
c. restricted
d. transferred
e. announced

3 **What can be inferred from the passage?**

a. Lincoln was not re-elected.
b. Lincoln was a great military leader.
c. Lincoln had excellent debating skills.
d. Lincoln wanted to stay in Illinois forever.
e. Lincoln's parents had close ties with politicians in Washington.

4 **What is the style of the passage?**

a. dry
b. biased
c. factual
d. nostalgic
e. whimsical

5 **Which best fits in the blanks?**

	(A)		(B)
a.	In fact	⋯	who
b.	Therefore	⋯	what
c.	However	⋯	that
d.	Furthermore	⋯	whom
e.	For example	⋯	which

A Words

A1. Fill in the blank according to the definition.

| independence | unjust | outrage | return | massacre |

1 _____: the action of killing many people all at once

2 _____: to come back to a place where you were before

3 _____: to make someone feel extremely angry and shocked

4 _____: freedom from the control, influence, or the like by another country

5 _____: not fair, especially because everyone doesn't have an equal opportunity

A2. Choose the most appropriate word for each blank.

1 The acrobat _____ walked across the tightrope without falling.
   a. unusually   b. deftly   c. clumsily   d. hardly

2 At a formal dinner, we should _____ proper etiquette at all times.
   a. practice   b. notice   c. conceal   d. reveal

3 Governments in some countries often _____ civil rights leaders to silence them.
   a. enslave   b. examine   c. silence   d. imprison

4 The government of Cuba is _____, so many Cubans try to escape.
   a. fair   b. complicated   c. oppressive   d. inscrutable

5 As children become adults, their parents gradually begin to _____ control of their lives.
   a. vanish   b. relegate   c. vanquish   d. relinquish

A3. Complete each sentence with one of the words from the box.

| flexible | assassinate | threatened | steady | oppose |

1 My schedule is _____, so I can take some time off next week.

2 I _____ the plan to build a freeway through our neighborhood.

3 A(n) _____ rain for about a week would be great for our struggling crops.

4 A gunman tried to _____ the prime minister on a recent state visit to Kuwait.

5 Owing to commercial whaling, many of the world's whale species are _____ with extinction.

B Expressions and Phrases

B1. Fill in the blank using an expression from the box.

by this time	under the law	once again	upon her return

1 All citizens should be treated equally _____.

2 _____ next week, they'll be in Rio de Janeiro.

3 _____, the entrance exam results of the college have been delayed!

4 _____ from Africa, she began to volunteer for the poor and orphan children.

B2. Complete each sentence with an expression from the reading passages.
(Change the form of the verb if necessary.)

rip apart	cooperate with	call for	be related to

1 Protestors _____ a ban on beef import last month.

2 You should _____ the police if they ever ask for your help.

3 She always _____ her credit card statements after paying them.

4 In the past, many people believed that education level _____ income.

C Summary

Complete the summary with the appropriate words and expressions.

won	admiration	rose	resistance
gave up	figure	accomplished	reunited	violence

Mahatma Gandhi won the _____ of the world because of his leadership in India. He was an important _____ in guiding India to independence from Britain. He encouraged the Indian people not to use _____. Instead, they showed _____ to the British rule in more peaceful ways, and in 1947, the UK _____ control.

Abraham Lincoln _____ from humble beginnings to become one of the greatest American presidents. After several other jobs, he _____ the presidential election. His leadership in the Civil War _____ the country, and he also made history by emancipating the slaves. Although he _____ many things, he was assassinated shortly after the war.

HOW WASTE CAN HELP US

Got Worms?

Pre-reading Activity

How can you reduce waste? Read and rank the following suggestions
from 1 (most important) to 5 (least important).

Don't get fast food "to go." _____   Don't use plastic bags.   _____
Recycle old newspapers.   _____   Use e-books and not regular books. _____

Traditionally, food waste has simply been tossed out with the trash. It   1
eventually makes its way to the local dump. However, some amateur—but very
innovative—gardeners have found a new way to dispose of food waste: worm
composting. Here's how it works. Place moist, shredded newspaper in a bin with
a number of earthworms. Then, instead of throwing food scraps in the garbage,   5
place them in the bin. The worms eat the scraps, essentially causing the food
waste to be broken down so that it is unrecognizable.

However, this is only the beginning. As they eat their way through the
scraps, <u>they</u> of course excrete some waste of their own. This worm manure is
very useful: it serves as nutrient-rich fertilizer, which can be used in gardens, on   10
lawns, or in potted plants. Once enough worm manure has been produced, it can
be harvested for use. Then new bedding of shredded newspaper is put in the bin,
and the process starts over.

Though worm composting is a great way to reduce waste, it is important to
keep in mind that not all food waste is appropriate for the worms. For example,   15
meats, oils, and dairy products should be avoided, as they are complex and don't
break down easily. Citrus fruit peels, onions, and broccoli contain natural
chemicals and enzymes that <u>disrupt</u> the composting process. Suitable scraps
include coffee grounds and paper filters, teabags, plate scraps, rotting fruit,
vegetable peelings, leftovers, and moldy bread. Worm composting may sound   20
gross, but it is a natural form of recycling. Moreover, it's an excellent way to
reduce garbage. Best of all, it helps in <u>growing healthier fruits and
vegetables locally</u> rather than buying older ones from
places far away.

Reading Tips

usage of "break down"

1. to stop working
   My car just broke down.

2. to hit something hard so that it
   falls down
   We had to break down the door to
   get into the room.

3. to start crying
   When she heard the news, she broke
   down.

4. to separate into the parts
   It was broken down by bacteria.

1   What is the main idea of the passage?

a. ways to dispose of food waste

b. how worms can help recycle food scraps

c. what worms eat and what worms don't eat

d. using recycling products to reduce garbage

e. how we can grow healthier fruits and vegetables

2   What does the word "they" refer to?

a. scraps

b. gardeners

c. local people

d. earthworms

e. fruits and vegetables

3   Which of the following is true?

a. Worms eat all of the food waste.

b. Worms eat layers of old newspaper.

c. Worms break down food waste by eating it.

d. Worms create heat energy by eating food scraps.

e. Worms eat too much food, die, and then are useful as fertilizer.

4   Which is closest in meaning to the word "disrupt"?

a. interrupt

b. organize

c. dislocate

d. rupture

e. serve

5   Why does the author mention growing vegetables locally?

a. It increases local air pollution.

b. It produces more organic waste.

c. It is good exercise because it is hard work.

d. It assists in cultivating beautiful lawns and flowers.

e. Less transportation means fresher fruits and vegetables.

Fill'er Up and Order of Fries, Please!

Pre-reading Activity

1. What kind of fuels can vehicles use? _____

2. What kind of plants are used for oil? _____

Scientists are hard at work trying to come up with viable alternative fuels to 1
power the world's vehicles. Many ideas have been <u>put forth</u>, including ethanol,
hydrogen, and even compressed air. One idea, however, may surprise many
people: vegetable oil. No stranger to the world's supermarkets and kitchens,
common vegetable oil may soon be found at gas stations. 5

Though the notion of using vegetable oil to run cars has only recently gained
much press, the theory was first tested in the early 1900s. At the time, it was done
as a publicity stunt at the 1900 World's Fair. Back then, replacing typical gasoline
with vegetable oil was unnecessary. However, now that the negative effects of
using traditional oils have become very apparent, vegetable oil is beginning to 10
look like a realistic alternative fuel.

Not all engines can run on vegetable oil. However, it is suitable for use in
many diesel engines. They often need only a slight modification to burn vegetable
oil. In most cases, the engine just needs to heat the oil a little before burning it.

There are currently two types of vegetable oil in regular use. (1) The first, 15
pure vegetable oil is simply oil straight from the plant or the bottle. (2)
The second, and far more interesting, is waste vegetable oil, which is
a by-product of the oil used in industrial deep fryers. (3) Just think:
after the local McDonald's cooks your French fries, you can use the
leftover oil to run your car. (4) But there could possibly be another 20
unintended side effect. (5) In the near future, instead of coughing
from inhaling dirty car exhaust every time you step outside, you
just might get the munchies.

Reading Tips

phrasal verbs with "put"

put up with: to accept an
unpleasant situation or person in
a patient way
She couldn't put up with their bad
behavior.

put on: to wear something
Sally put on her hat before leaving the
house.

put down: to criticize someone
John is always trying to put her down.

1   **What is the passage mainly about?**

a. eating at the gas station

b. using vegetable oil as fuel

c. fueling up at the fast food restaurant

d. presenting new car engine technology

e. the process of developing alternative fuels

2   **Which is closest in meaning to the phrase "put forth"?**

a. ruled out

b. proposed

c. thought of

d. eliminated

e. forgotten about

3   **Which of the following is true?**

a. Hybrid cars run on vegetable oil.

b. There is no problem using vegetable oil in car engines.

c. In the early 1900s, using vegetable oil as fuel was popular.

d. Using vegetable oil as an alternative fuel will not have any side effect.

e. Not only pure vegetable oil but also waste vegetable oil can be used as fuel.

4   **Where does the following sentence best fit in the passage?**

It is a novel use of oil that would have otherwise gone to waste.

a. (1)

b. (2)

c. (3)

d. (4)

e. (5)

5   **What are the two types of vegetable oil in regular use?**

A Words

A1. Fill in the blank according to the definition.

citrus	leftovers	alternative	viable	gross

1 _____: food that remains at the end of a meal
2 _____: very unpleasant to taste, smell, see, or feel
3 _____: category of fruit including lemons and oranges
4 _____: able to be done successfully such as an idea or plan
5 _____: another choice or option which can be used instead of something

A2. Choose the most appropriate word for each blank.

1 Don't _____ the fumes, or you'll have a splitting headache!
  a. drink   b. look at   c. inhale   d. touch

2 Let's leave for the airport now; _____, we might miss our plane.
  a. until   b. tomorrow   c. nevertheless   d. otherwise

3 His lack of sleep was _____ from his red eyes and appearance.
  a. apparent   b. belated   c. characteristic   d. devious

4 In summer, you can smell _____ garbage from the town dump from far away.
  a. low   b. rolling   c. tall   d. rotting

5 You should _____ your bank statements to protect your personal information.
  a. share   b. shred   c. shriek   d. stare

A3. Complete each sentence with one of the words from the box.

harvested	essentially	unrecognizable	moist	appropriate

1 She's _____ as the girl I once knew in my childhood.
2 Barley is usually planted in early October and _____ in June.
3 The government should take _____ action if the union goes on strike.
4 My younger brother is _____ a vegetarian, but he eats meat sometimes.
5 Earthworms always have to keep their skin _____ because they breathe through their skin.

B

Expressions and Phrases

B1. Fill in the blank using an expression from the box.

now that	best of all	in the near future	in most cases

1 I do not plan to visit Europe or the U.S. _____.

2 _____, stolen items are not found by the police.

3 _____ you are here, please make yourself comfortable.

4 There are many positive things about winning lottery. _____,
I can buy a bigger house.

**B2. Complete each sentence with an expression from the reading passages.
(Change the form of the verb if necessary.)**

toss out	break down	keep in mind	come up with

1 I need to _____ a good reason why my homework is not done yet.

2 You should be in class on time. Please _____ that _____.

3 His car _____ on the freeway during rush hour on Monday morning.

4 She accidentally _____ some important papers _____ with the trash.

C

Summary

Complete the summary with the appropriate words and expressions.

garbage	run on	alternative	broken down
recycling	fertilizer	cut down	dependence

Worm composting is a way of _____ food scraps instead of throwing them out
with local trash. Most such waste goes into garbage dumps. However, feeding leftover food
to earthworms allows it to be _____. The resulting compost is a very rich type
of _____. Using it will reduce _____ and will enable fresh, healthy
vegetables to be grown locally.

Recycled vegetable oil could be a viable _____ to gasoline. It has been used
as a fuel for many years, and diesel car engines are easy to convert so that they will
_____ vegetable oil. This could reduce the world's _____ on
petroleum, and it would _____ on air pollution.

SURVIVOR STORIES
Four Days in the Desert

Pre-reading Activity

What is the largest desert in the world, and what continent is it on?

_____

In your opinion what is the most dangerous place to be stranded?

desert   ocean   deserted island   mountain

The McDonald family from Glasgow, Scotland, was on holiday in Western 1
Australia when their vehicle broke down in a <u>rugged</u> desert region ninety miles
north of the town of Laverton. This happened on a Tuesday, and the McDonalds
were expected to arrive in the city of Kalgoorlie on Wednesday evening. When
they did not show up, Mrs. McDonald's brother notified the local police.   5

A spokesperson from the rescue team that discovered the McDonalds'
vehicle said that the family was well-prepared for their desert trek. They knew
that they needed to stay with their vehicle instead of setting out to seek help, and
they did the right thing by lighting a fire to attract attention. Sensible precautions
would include bringing warm clothing for the cold nights and light clothing, hats, 10
and sunscreen for the hot days. _____, travelers should have a well-stocked
survival kit including a first-aid kit, map, matches or lighter, and a knife. They
should also make sure to pack plenty of food and water, spare tires, and fuel. The
spokesperson's final recommendation was to tell a friend or family member about
your travel plans.   15

After the ordeal, John McDonald told reporters that he had read extensively
about desert survival before coming to Australia. He knew that if they had
attempted to walk to the nearest town, they would not be able to carry enough
water. Mrs. McDonald made sure that the family drank water and reduced what
they ate, because digestion requires a great deal of water.   20

Mr. McDonald said he was profoundly relieved to see the
rescue team and grateful that his family had survived. When asked
what advice he could share with other prospective desert travelers, Mr.
McDonald said, "Don't panic. Stay calm and wait to be rescued." This trek
through the Australian outback is one vacation the McDonald family will
never forget!

Reading Tips

usage of "light"

noun: brightness from the sun, a flame, a lamp, which allows you to see things
I opened the curtains to let the light in.

adjective: not heavy
I want to buy a light bag.

verb: to make something start to burn
I lit the candle.

1 What is the main idea of the passage?

   a. giving tourists tips on visiting Western Australia
   b. giving instructions on surviving in harsh conditions
   c. providing details on how to prepare for desert travel
   d. explaining the various ways people can die in the desert
   e. giving an account of how the McDonald family survived in the desert

2 Which is closest in meaning to the word "rugged"?

   a. dry
   b. rocky
   c. sandy
   d. rough
   e. smooth

3 What can be inferred from the passage?

   a. We need a special vehicle for crossing a desert.
   b. Those who want to cross a desert need a trained tour guide.
   c. If you get lost in a desert, look for a place where you can get help.
   d. In Australia, many people get lost while crossing the desert in summer.
   e. The difference of temperature between day and night is sharp in the desert.

4 Which best fits in the blank?

   a. So
   b. However
   c. Therefore
   d. In contrast
   e. Furthermore

5 What did the McDonald family do when their car broke down in a desert?

Nerves of Steel

02

Pre-reading Activity

Look at the title of the passage and write down five words you think will be in the passage.

_____ _____ _____ _____ _____

Now scan the passage and see if you were right. How many? _____

What does it mean to have nerves of steel? How does one remain in control   1
when his/her life and the lives of many others are on the line? U.S. Airways pilot,
Chesley B. "Sully" Sullenberger, demonstrated this poise and emerged as a hero
when he smoothly landed his commercial airliner on the Hudson River.

(1) Just minutes after taking off from New York's LaGuardia Airport on   5
January 15, 2009, Sullenberger's Airbus A-320 found itself in dire straits. (2)
The pilot quickly contacted air traffic control to find an available runway on
which to land his <u>crippled</u> aircraft. (3) His message rang out over the airwaves,
"Hit birds, we lost thrust in both engines, we're turning back to LaGuardia." (4)
The controllers scrambled to find a runway for U.S. Airways Flight 1549. (5)   10
The captain made a lightning-fast decision and announced: "We may end up in
the Hudson." On board the plane, panicky passengers heard the captain's steady
voice say, "Brace for impact." Tensions ran high on the aircraft as passengers put
their lives into the hands of a stranger.

Later, the pilot told the Federal Aviation Administration investigators that he   15
glided the plane into the river rather than risk a catastrophic crash in a densely-
populated area. Fortunately, ferries were in the vicinity, and all 155 people aboard
were rescued. Passengers had nothing but praise for the skilled airbus driver. As
for Sullenberger, he told interviewers that he was just doing his job.

Sullenberger became an American hero the day he landed in the Hudson   20
River. He was received and congratulated by President Barack Obama. A
ceremony for Sullenberger was held on January 24, 2009, in his hometown
of Danville, California, where he was presented with an award and
named an honorary police officer for his heroics. Thank
goodness he had years of practice and nerves   25
of steel!

Reading Tips

usage of "take off"

1. to remove clothes or something you're wearing
   You should take off your shoes inside the house.

2. to start flying
   The plane didn't take off on time.

3. to become successful very fast
   Rachel's career started taking off.

4. to have a holiday from work
   I'm taking Friday off.

5. to leave
   You just missed Jane. She just took off.

1 What is the main idea of the passage?

a. discussing aviation safety
b. talking about the airline U.S. Airways
c. explaining the phrase "nerves of steel"
d. discussing ways to survive a plane crash
e. telling the story of the pilot Chesley Sullenberger

2 Which is closest in meaning to the word "crippled"?

a. full
b. elected
c. swollen
d. damaged
e. dangerous

3 What is the author's attitude toward Chesley Sullenberger?

a. admiring
b. negative
c. hopeful
d. neutral
e. factual

4 What is the purpose of the passage?

a. to alarm the reader
b. to talk about problems with U.S. Airways
c. to discuss Chesley Sullenberger's heroic landing
d. to make the reader aware of an airline safety problem
e. to change the reader's mind about flying into New York airports

5 Where does the following sentence best fit in the passage?

> However, there was not enough time to get back to LaGuardia.

a. (1)   b. (2)   c. (3)   d. (4)   e. (5)

A Words

A1. Fill in the blank according to the definition.

| notify | spokesperson | relieved | seek | poise |

1 _____: to inform or tell
2 _____: to try to locate or discover; to inquire for
3 _____: a representative of a group, organization, or government
4 _____: feeling better after something bad or uncomfortable is over
5 _____: a calm and relaxed way of behaving, even in difficult situations

A2. Choose the most appropriate word for each blank.

1 The athlete was _____ after a terrible skiing accident.
   a. confident   b. understood   c. crippled   d. refreshed

2 The plane is making a(n) _____ climb toward its cruising altitude.
   a. eventual   b. downward   c. upfront   d. steady

3 When the stock market crashed, most investors were _____.
   a. panicky   b. relaxed   c. dangerous   d. uninterested

4 I need a massage, because there is a lot of _____ in my neck.
   a. contusion   b. slackness   c. tension   d. sadness

5 I am _____ for your kindness and hospitality.
   a. studying   b. confused   c. unhappy   d. grateful

A3. Complete each sentence with one of the words from the box.

| ordeal | sensible | precaution | investigator | risk |

1 I took a big _____ when I invested in a new company.
2 It is not very _____ to go outdoors in winter without a coat on.
3 The private _____ discovered many interesting facts for his client.
4 When our cruise ship hit an iceberg and sank, it was an awful _____!
5 As a(n) _____, you should get vaccinated before visiting another country.

B Expressions and Phrases

B1. Fill in the blank using an expression in the box.

on holiday	a great deal of	in the vicinity	nothing but

1 Bucheon is a city located _____ of Seoul.

2 I have spent _____ money fixing up my new house.

3 While I am _____, I do not want to think about my job.

4 We can do _____ wait for rescue in the center of the storm.

B2. Complete each sentence with an expression from the reading passages.
   (Change the form of the verb if necessary.)

end up	show up	make sure	take off

1 Why did you _____ without an invitation to this party?

2 Let's _____ we don't forget our passports and plane tickets!

3 I'm supposed to check in two hours before the plane _____.

4 After the bribery scandal surfaced, the prime minister _____ resigning.

C Summary

Complete the summary with the appropriate words and expressions.

take-off	supplies	prepared	decision
stranded	turn back	rescuers	prevented

The McDonald family from Scotland was _____ in the desert of Western Australia after their car broke down. Fortunately, they had _____ well for their trip. They had the correct _____, and they stayed near their car and lit a signal fire. This enabled _____ to find them safe and alive.

The U.S. Airways pilot Chesley Sullenberger made a quick _____ that saved many people's lives. Both engines failed after the plane hit a flock of birds shortly after _____ from a New York City airport. There was no time to _____, so he landed in the Hudson River. This _____ a terrible crash in the city and saved not just his passengers but many others as well.

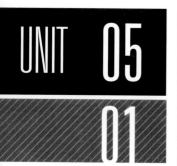

LANGUAGES

Bringing Back "Aloha"

Pre-reading Activity

From the languages below, choose the three most useful ones and rank them.

French   Chinese   Japanese   English   German   Spanish

1st _____   2nd _____   3rd _____

In Hawaii, there are two official languages: English and Hawaiian. The ⒈ Hawaiian language is very similar to languages spoken across the Pacific Ocean in places like Fiji and the Philippines. The Hawaiian language came very close to becoming an <u>extinct</u> language, though.

A number of factors were involved with the decline of the Hawaiian ⒌ language. First of all, the arrival of explorers in the late 1700s and missionaries in the early 1800s brought not only new cultures and ideas, but diseases as well. Many locals died because they had no immunity to those diseases. The number of native Hawaiian speakers fell rapidly. Second, the Hawaiian monarchy was overthrown and in 1896, English became the official language of schools ⒑ and government. With an increasing American presence, English became the language of business, further limiting the use of Hawaiian. Year after year, the sounds of the native language became less common in the streets.

When Hawaii became one of the United States in 1959, the people fought to have Hawaiian included as an official language. Now, more and more Hawaiians ⒖ are trying to learn their ancestral language, and the Hawaiian state government is attempting to help them. Hawaiian classes are now taught in the schools, Hawaiian newspapers are published, and there are some Hawaiian radio shows. A new dictionary of the language was even created. One particularly novel way the government is trying to protect the language is by <u>not allowing tourism to the island of Niihau</u>. There, ⒛ Hawaiian is the only language spoken by the residents!

Although Hawaiian has been saved from extinction, it is spoken by only 1.5% of the population. Japanese and the Filipino language Tagalog are in much wider use in the Hawaiian Islands. The Hawaiian language still has a long way to go. If you visit, though, you might hear people using the Hawaiian word "aloha" instead of "hello."

Reading Tips

expressions with "number of"

a number of + plural noun: many people or things
<u>A number of teenagers</u> <u>have</u> part-time jobs in the U.S.A.

the number of + plural noun: the quantity of people or things
<u>The number of immigrants</u> <u>is</u> increasing rapidly.

1   **What is the main idea of the passage?**

a. exploring the political status of Hawaii

b. discussing the languages used in Hawaii

c. giving a history of the extinction of the Hawaiian language

d. comparing and contrasting Tagalog, Japanese, and Hawaiian

e. explaining the background and status of the Hawaiian language

2   **Which is closest in meaning to the word "extinct"?**

a. dead

b. living

c. thriving

d. reduced

e. dwindling

3   **Which of the following is not true?**

a. Other languages except English are spoken in Hawaii.

b. The Hawaiian language is an official language in Hawaii.

c. Since 1959, the number of Hawaiians using their language has decreased.

d. The state government tries to keep the Hawaiian language from becoming extinct.

e. Diseases that came from western countries caused the native Hawaiian speakers to decline.

4   **What is the author's attitude toward the resurgence of the Hawaiian language?**

a. indifferent

b. optimistic

c. callous

d. neutral

e. amused

5   **Why does the author mention the tourism restriction on the island of Niihau?**

a. to imply that Niihau is not part of Hawaii

b. to imply that Niihau is an unattractive island for tourists

c. to suggest that too much English is being used on Niihau

d. to suggest that the language of Niihau is different from Hawaiian

e. to show that Hawaii's government is taking strong steps to protect the language

Hieroglyphics

Pre-reading Activity

True or False?

1. T – F: All pyramids are located in Egypt.
2. T – F: The word "hieroglyphics" means "picture words."
3. T – F: Hieroglyphics was the form of writing used in ancient Egypt.

Most people have seen a picture of the Egyptian pyramids, or the Sphinx, but does anyone know what all the little drawings inside the pyramids mean? For centuries, the Egyptian language was a mystery. It took a lot of luck and study for people to finally <u>crack</u> the code of Egyptian hieroglyphics.

The word hieroglyphics means "divine words," or "language of the gods." Egyptian hieroglyphs first began as pictures of things people saw every day: plants, animals, buildings, and people. Later on, those pictures became a spoken and written language. Egyptian is one of the oldest languages in the world and was spoken for about 5,000 years. However, in the 10th and 11th centuries, the Egyptian language died out: it was replaced by the Arabic language, and all understanding of the hieroglyphs was lost.

An understanding of Egyptian hieroglyphs was made possible only by the lucky discovery of the Rosetta Stone. The Rosetta Stone was found in 1799, near the city of Alexandria, by a soldier in the French army. On the Rosetta Stone is writing from three different languages: Egyptian hieroglyphics, Egyptian demotic writing, and Greek. The importance of the stone was that the exact same message was written in the three different languages. Historians could read the message in Greek and then read the same message in hieroglyphics. With the Rosetta Stone, they could begin to understand all Egyptian hieroglyphics.

In 1824, Jean-François Champollion published a book about the hieroglyphs and won a number of awards for cracking the hieroglyph code. However, many other people helped, and the whole process of understanding took several years. Today, professors around the world are using Champollion's book to read Egyptian writing. You can, too! Check online to see how you can read the walls of a mummy's tomb, or send a secret message in Egyptian hieroglyphics.

Reading Tips

usage of "colon (:)"

1. to introduce particular lists
She has three brothers: John, James, and Justin.

2. to introduce a clause that interprets or amplifies the first
Accommodations in Manhattan are pretty expensive: the average price of a moderate hotel is over $200 per night.

3. to introduce a quotation
Albert Einstein said: "Before God we are all equally wise- and equally foolish."

1   What is the main idea of the passage?

a. a lesson on the history of Ancient Egypt
b. the way pictures became a form of writing
c. comparing hieroglyphics with other writing systems
d. a translation lesson between English and hieroglyphics
e. historical and background information on hieroglyphics

2   What is true about the Rosetta Stone?

a. It was written by Greek scholars.
b. It contained a dictionary of hieroglyphics.
c. It provided a translation into Egyptian demotic writing.
d. It showed the same text in both hieroglyphics and Greek.
e. It was written in the earliest form of the English language.

3   Which is closest in meaning to the word "crack"?

a. start
b. solve
c. smash
d. dissolve
e. question

4   Which best fits in the blanks?

For a long time, nobody could _____ Egyptian hieroglyphics. It was not _____ the Rosetta Stone was _____ that we could understand the Egyptian hieroglyphics.

a. find, till, read
b. decipher, until, found
c. locate, until, covered
d. understand, till, founded
e. read, before, established

5   What pictures were used first to write the ancient Egyptian language?

_____

A Words

A1. Fill in the blank according to the definition.

extinct	decline	attempt	allow	discovery

1 _____: to try to do something

2 _____: decrease in number or quality

3 _____: no longer active or alive; dead

4 _____: an act or the process of finding something

5 _____: to let someone do something; to give permission

A2. Choose the most appropriate word for each blank.

1 I've had this sofa for 10 years, so it's time to _____ it.
  a. assemble   b. pack   c. own   d. replace

2 My father is a _____ who specializes in Ancient Greek politics.
  a. doctor   b. historian   c. mayor   d. resident

3 When you _____ your first book, it's almost as exciting as having a baby.
  a. burn   b. eat   c. give away   d. publish

4 Although I have an American passport, legally I am a(n) _____ of Hong Kong.
  a. neighbor   b. resident   c. owner   d. consultant

5 I can't _____ you to watch TV until you have finished all your homework.
  a. forbid   b. allow   c. encourage   d. suggest

A3. Complete each sentence with one of the words from the box.

immunity	overthrow	presence	native	particularly

1 I'm not _____ fond of food made with a lot of garlic and pork.

2 I had chicken pox as a little kid, so I have a(n) _____ to the disease now.

3 My mother is a(n) _____ of Portugal, so I speak both English and Portuguese.

4 The rebels in the south of the country want to _____ the national government.

5 The U.S.A. has a large military _____ in Korea, Germany, and several other countries.

B Expressions and Phrases

B1. Fill in the blank using an expression in the box.

instead of	a number of	as well	year after year

1 I've read the book, and I've seen the movie _____.

2 Jane was given bail by the judge _____ being sent to jail.

3 Some traditions in our culture have been passed down _____.

4 _____ people think that Turkey should not join the European Union.

B2. Complete each sentence with an expression from the reading passages.
   (Change the form of the verb if necessary.)

come close to	be involved with	be in use	die out

1 The telegraph _____ until the telephone was invented.

2 I _____ an activist group as a student, but as an adult I'm too busy.

3 She had cancer and _____ dying, but a new treatment saved her life.

4 We don't know why the dinosaurs _____ millions and millions of years ago.

C Summary

Complete the summary with the appropriate words and expressions.

official	restored	interpret	bearing
extinct	comprehension	replaced	related

The Hawaiian language, which is _____ to languages in the Philippines and Fiji, almost became _____. When Europeans arrived on the islands, many Hawaiians perished. English became the _____ language of school and government. Fortunately, after Hawaii became a state, Hawaiian was _____ as one of its official languages.

Hieroglyphics are the written form of the extinct Egyptian language, which was _____ by Arabic about 1,000 years ago. For centuries, no one could read hieroglyphics. When the Rosetta Stone—a tablet _____ the same message in hieroglyphics, Egyptian demotic writing, and Greek—was found, scholars could _____ the hieroglyphics. Our _____ of hieroglyphics today all happened because of the Rosetta Stone!

CHANGING MEDIA

Reality Television

Pre-reading Activity

How much TV do you watch per day? _____

What kind of TV programs do you watch most? _____

In recent years, reality television has become very popular. There are ₁ reality television programs to <u>suit</u> almost every interest: interior design, fashion, music, cooking, dancing, and many others. The popularity and profitability of reality programs for television networks are something that no one can refute. Its legitimacy as worthwhile programming, on the other hand, is an often-debated ₅ topic.

Reality television has been with us since about 1948, when a prankster started filming practical jokes he played on strangers. From such a modest beginning, it had changed into something entirely different by the early 1990's. Today reality programs rely on humiliation and conflict as a way to create ₁₀ excitement. Though the programs aren't necessarily scripted, the producers intentionally select people of different backgrounds and ideologies to create tension. This tension creates excitement for the viewers. It comes in the form of violence, arguments, hysterics, and other questionable behavior. When viewers watch the participants act, it sends a message to viewers that what they are seeing ₁₅ is normal, appropriate behavior. In the end, reality television may be helping to create a crude and selfish society.

In the past, people were happy with simply making jokes and having a good time on television. ___(A)___ reality television stays on the air, ___(B)___ outrageous it gets. With every passing season, the producers look for new ways to increase ₂₀ the ratings. Today, viewers expect to see physical fighting at least once in a season. At the current rate of escalation, one can only imagine what will be required to achieve high ratings in the future. The only way for us to put a stop to this and protect our society is by putting an end to reality television.

25

Reading Tips

though / although

conjunction: used to introduce a statement that makes the main statement coming after it seem surprising, unlikely, or unexpected
• Though I missed the train at six, I arrived at the meeting on time.
• Although she is very young, she is intelligent.

in spite of / despite

preposition: without being affected or prevented by something
• In spite of everything, we still enjoyed our vacation.
• He didn't take off his coat, despite the heat.

1   What is the main idea of the passage?

a. TV's bad influence on teenagers
b. a call for more reality TV shows
c. violence and bad behavior on reality TV
d. reality television and its effect on society
e. comparing reality TV with other types of TV programming

2   Which is closest in meaning to the word "suit"?

a. do
b. hurt
c. wear
d. crave
e. satisfy

3   What can be inferred from the passage?

a. Nowadays most people watch TV too much.
b. Teenagers imitate reality TV shows' participants.
c. Social scientists are in favor of reality TV shows.
d. The deliberate plot of reality TV influences society.
e. Television has little influence upon public behavior.

4   What is the author's attitude toward reality television?

a. critical
b. neutral
c. positive
d. supportive
e. sympathetic

5   Which best fits in the blanks?

	(A)		(B)
a.	The more	···	the better
b.	The longer	···	the more
c.	The longer	···	the less
d.	The more	···	the less
e.	The less	···	the longer

Gossip Media

Pre-reading Activity

Fill in the blanks using the words *paparazzi* and *celebrity*.

_____ take photos of celebrities at moments when they do not expect to be photographed.

A _____ is widely-recognized or notable person in a society or culture.

A glimpse at a newspaper, the Internet, or a TV newscast makes it easy to see that public figures don't have much privacy. Every day there is juicy new gossip to be consumed, and the stories are often accompanied by <u>compromising</u> pictures and sometimes video. The gossip sector of media has become its own industry, and it is big business.

When there is such widespread attraction to something, there are always those who criticize it. In this case, people are asking ___(A)___ the media has the right to publicly announce private information about famous individuals. However, some argue that movie stars and other entertainers have made a conscious decision to go into public life. In today's world, there is very little privacy. Juicy photos and stories about celebrities can be worth a lot of money, and the paparazzi have been snapping pictures for a long time. One could even say that this is the price to pay for fame.

There is also a bit of hypocrisy involved in the situation. Most of these celebrities and socialites actively pursued the media to gain exposure early in their careers. It was a strategy for advancement in their careers. Many also sought fame by intentionally revealing personal information, if it meant getting a story written about them. Their attitudes changed once they became famous. Suddenly the media became a nuisance, and these stars wanted their privacy.

The gossip media is doing a public service by reporting on celebrities. The evidence is in the popularity of gossip media. People are interested and fascinated by the lifestyles of the rich and famous. ___(B)___ the celebrities are uncomfortable with the idea of becoming fodder for gossip, then the solution is simple: they shouldn't seek out a job in the limelight.

1

5

10

15

20

25

Reading Tips

phrasal verbs with "make"

make up: to combine together to form something
The book is made up of fifteen separate short stories.

make out: to see, hear, or understand someone or something
Can you make out what she was saying?

make it: to manage to arrive on time
If you leave now, you'll make it before the train leaves.

1   **What is the passage mainly about?**

a. who the paparazzi are

b. people who want privacy

c. the gossip media and why it exists

d. the gossip media industry and its future

e. encouraging people to conceal their personal information

2   **Which is closest in meaning to the word "compromising"?**

a. dirty

b. exciting

c. agreeing

d. bargaining

e. embarrassing

3   **Which best fits in the blanks?**

(A)		(B)
a. how	⋯	As
b. why	⋯	When
c. when	⋯	Although
d. whether	⋯	If
e. that	⋯	Because

4   **What advice does the author have for potential celebrities?**

a. Buy the fastest car you can afford and hire a bodyguard.

b. Become a writer, not an actor or singer. No one cares about writers.

c. If you don't want to be pursued by reporters, stay out of Los Angeles.

d. If you don't like the paparazzi, stay out of show business.

e. Wear a mask, sunglasses, and a wig at all times.

5   **Why do some people criticize celebrity gossip magazines and websites?**

Unit Review

A Words

A1. Fill in the blank according to the definition.

refute	prankster	modest	conscious	celebrity

1 _____: to say that a statement is not true

2 _____: awake; noticing or realizing something

3 _____: a person who likes to play jokes on others

4 _____: a famous person, especially in entertainment or sport

5 _____: preferring not to talk about his or her own strengths or good qualities

A2. Choose the most appropriate word for each blank.

1 Paris Hilton is perhaps today's most famous example of a _____.

   a. time bomb   b. socialite   c. social climber   d. volunteer

2 _____ to radiation is known to cause cancer.

   a. Exposure   b. Illness   c. Oxygen   d. Deprivation

3 The officer was forced to _____ secrets to the enemy.

   a. terminate   b. collide   c. deny   d. reveal

4 The police found a lot of _____ that Mr. Smith had really stolen the money.

   a. testament   b. conviction   c. evidence   d. guilt

5 When two celebrities spend time together, it is always _____ for gossip.

   a. fodder   b. petroleum   c. lubrication   d. tonic

A3. Complete each sentence with one of the words from the box.

fame	pursue	tension	outrageous	hysterics

1 The price of gasoline these days is just _____!

2 Many young people move to Hollywood every year, seeking _____.

3 This high level talk will help ease _____ between the two countries.

4 I hope the police will _____ the escaped criminals until they are all found.

5 When my sister heard she had won the contest, she jumped up and down in _____.

B Expressions and Phrases

B1. Fill in the blank using an expression in the box.

on the other hand	in the end	for a long time	a bit of

1 When you fly to Australia, you are in the plane _____.
2 Could I have _____ ice in my coffee, please? It's very hot.
3 Things may be difficult now, but everything will be fine _____.
4 I think I want a blueberry muffin for breakfast, but _____, those chocolate ones look good, too.

B2. Complete each sentence with an expression from the reading passages.
   (Change the form of the verb if necessary.)

put an end to	seek out	make a decision	pay for

1 It's hard to _____ when everybody is staring at me!
2 One of the most efficient ways to _____ snoring is surgery.
3 We don't have enough money to _____ the gas and mortgage.
4 When you move to a new city, it is important to _____ a group of friends.

C Summary

Complete the summary with the appropriate words and expressions.

negative	critics	reveal	interest
privacy	profitable	humiliation	specializes

Many people seem to like reality TV shows, and there is a program for every _____.
They are also very _____ for the TV networks. The first reality shows were just simple pranks and jokes, but today the shows rely on fights, _____, and outrageous behavior. They are having a _____ effect on society.

A whole section of the news media _____ in gossip and juicy pictures of famous people. People love to read these stories and see the pictures, but there are also _____. Should the media _____ personal details about celebrities? Perhaps this loss of _____ is the price that people pay for fame.

REMARKABLE ANIMALS

Chameleons

Pre-reading Activity

True or False?

1. T – F: Chameleons have good vision.
2. T – F: Chameleons are found in Africa.
3. T – F: Chameleons are difficult to spot.
4. T – F: Chameleons change their color only for protection.

The chameleon is a type of lizard and is best-known for its ability to change   1
colors. In addition to this fascinating ability, chameleons have distinctive,
complex tongues that are used to catch prey. Chameleons also have independently
mobile eyes. Unlike humans, whose eyes cannot move independently, chameleons
can look in two directions at once! Chameleons are found in Africa, parts of   5
Europe, Asia, and North America. Although they require warm climates, they are
found in rainforests as well as deserts.

There are a number of reasons why chameleons change colors. Chameleons'
ability to blend in with their surroundings has made many people fascinated with
them. Some species of chameleons—but not all—possess a layer of specialized   10
cells that make this color shift possible. The most obvious use for the color
change is for camouflage. Chameleons can   (A)   to most of the hues found
in nature: green, brown, black, grey, cream, and yellow. Some can turn orange,
pink, or red with no difficulty. Others develop very complex patterns as well.
This makes them difficult for predators to <u>spot</u>, but it is not the only reason for   15
the color changes.

For certain chameleons, color serves as an indicator
of the animal's physiological state. If the chameleon is
angry or frightened, if it has been victorious in a fight,
or if it is searching for a mate, it might change colors.
These color changes are not voluntary; however, it happens
as a reflex. Chameleons have powerful vision, too. The lenses
of their eyes can magnify things like a camera's telephoto lens.
They can see ultraviolet light, too. Because they are able to detect
   (B)   variations in color, they developed this powerful signaling system.   25
Some scientists believe that this ability came first, and the ability to use color
as a form of protective camouflage came later.

Reading Tips

like: similar to someone or
something else
(preposition + noun)
Her hair is curly blond like my sister.

unlike: different from someone or
something else
(preposition + noun)
*Unlike my brother, I often get up
early.*

alike: (adjective) very similar;
          (adverb) in a similar way
• *My grandmother and my dad are
alike in many ways.*
• *His siblings were all dressed alike.*

1 **What is the passage mainly about?**

a. how chameleons shift colors

b. why chameleons change colors

c. where chameleons can be found

d. the native habitat of the chameleon

e. chameleons and their color-shifting abilities

2 **Which is closest in meaning to the word "spot"?**

a. discover

b. catch

c. hunt

d. run

e. dot

3 **Which best fits in the blanks?**

(A)		(B)
a. adopt	...	delicate
b. identify	...	enormous
c. modify	...	huge
d. adapt	...	subtle
e. search	...	little

4 **What can be inferred from the passage?**

a. Chameleons are predatory.

b. Chameleons' colors can change involuntarily.

c. Chameleons are not able to inhabit dry areas.

d. Chameleons change their colors only to protect themselves.

e. Movement of chameleons' eyes is the same as that of humans' eyes.

5 **Why does the author mention the different colors chameleons can display?**

a. to imply that other animals have the same ability

b. to state that one chameleon can display all these colors

c. to suggest that chameleons are not all the same species

d. to suggest that sometimes chameleons control a variety of colors

e. to show that chameleons' color change is limited by environment

REMARKABLE ANIMALS

Elephants

Pre-reading Activity

Fill in the blanks using the words *land*, *different*, *live*, and *distinguishing*.

Elephants are the largest _____ animals, and they usually _____ for 50 to 70 years. African elephants are _____ from Asian elephants in several ways, and the most noticeable _____ feature is their ears. African elephants have much larger ears.

The mind of an elephant should not be <u>underestimated</u>. They are brilliant creatures blessed with both excellent memory and artistic talent. Elephants consume approximately 495 pounds of vegetarian food a day. They spend about 16 hours a day eating, but must walk about 4 miles a day in search of food. This extreme need for food is a huge burden to the elephants. The average elephant lives approximately 70 years, and its sharp memory allows it to remember locations where it has found food as long as thirty years earlier, even as a baby.

In an elephant's travels, they come across other elephants also looking for food. Some elephants are friendly, and some are not so nice. Elephants remember every elephant they have ever met. They can even recognize an elephant whom they perhaps haven't seen for thirty years. They immediately remember whether this elephant is a threat or a potential friend.

When elephants are not searching for food, they sometimes produce art in the sand with their trunks. They seem to enjoy just relaxing and painting in the sand. One day, an elephant zoo-keeper noticed this and gave an elephant a paint brush filled with red paint to see what it would do. The zoo-keeper put a canvas on the ground to see _____ the elephant would paint on it. Sure enough, it did, and since then elephants in most zoos have been given paint brushes, paints, and canvases. The resulting abstract art has been sold for high prices around the world. The funds go to support feeding the elephants in the zoos. Most felt that the elephants were only capable of painting abstracts. However, they have been trained to paint trees, flowers, and other items in nature. This has enabled us to understand "elephant genius" even more.

1

5

10

15

20

25

Reading Tips

phrasal verbs with "come"

come up with: to think of an idea or a plan, etc.
I've been asked to come up with some new opinions.

come down with: to get an illness
I am coming down with the flu.

come by: to manage to get something
How did you come by Britney's new release?

1 What is the best alternative title of the passage?

a. The Artist of the Jungle
b. The Elephants' Graveyard
c. The Elephant: The Big Eater
d. The Intellectual Animal: the Elephant
e. The Hidden Stories of Elephants' Travels

2 Which is closest in meaning to the word "underestimated"?

a. criticized
b. evaluated
c. overvalued
d. undervalued
e. exaggerated

3 Which of the following is NOT true?

a. Elephants spend most of the day eating.
b. Elephants may walk a long way to find food.
c. An elephant may remember every elephant it has ever met.
d. An elephant's life span is much longer than that of a human being.
e. Elephants can remember places where they found food 30 years ago.

4 Which best fits in the blank?

a. if
b. that
c. while
d. which
e. although

5 Which best fits in the blanks?

Elephants are so smart that they can _____ an elephant that they met a long time ago. They also can draw pictures using their _____.

a. tell, ears   b. see, mouths
c. smell, noses   d. paint, eyes
e. recognize, trunks

A Words

A1. Fill in the blank according to the definition.

hue	indicator	physiological	threat	potential

1 _____: a variety of color

2 _____: relating to the body

3 _____: the possibility that something will gradually develop

4 _____: a situation or something that may cause harm or danger

5 _____: a sign or signal that shows what condition something is in

A2. Choose the most appropriate word for each blank.

1 His big glasses look funny because they _____ his eyes.

   a. absorb   b. wrinkle   c. enlighten   d. magnify

2 Many people think we will someday _____ life on other planets.

   a. overlook   b. display   c. detect   d. conclude

3 Jamie likes to pretend he is a little stupid so that people will _____ him.

   a. respect   b. underestimate   c. love   d. challenge

4 Jennifer moved out to the country because she wanted quieter _____.

   a. downtown   b. school   c. metropolitan   d. surroundings

5 Jane Austin's *Pride and Prejudice*, which is narrated in free indirect speech, is a(n) _____ novel.

   a. brilliant   b. unknown   c. obscene   d. simple

A3. Complete each sentence with one of the words from the box.

shift	adapted	camouflage	signal	extreme

1 These materials can be _____ to suit for younger children.

2 I like Seattle because it does not have _____ temperatures.

3 The earthquake caused the house to _____ on its foundation.

4 That look on your face is a clear _____ that you're in a bad mood.

5 The soldier's _____ uniform made him almost invisible in the forest.

B Expressions and Phrases

B1. Fill in the blank using an expression from the box.

in addition to	at once	as long as	in search of

1 The research shows us that men don't live _____ women.
2 They left the village _____ food, but they didn't return until today.
3 It's hard to follow a conversation when several people are talking _____.
4 _____ earthquakes, southern California also has terrible wildfires each year.

B2. Complete each sentence with an expression from the reading passages.
(Change the form of the verb if necessary.)

blend in with	come across	be capable of	be blessed with

1 I thought he _____ handling the project, but he wasn't.
2 I _____ my high school graduation photos while cleaning my desk.
3 When my friend and I travel, we try to _____ the crowd, as it's safer.
4 Though Bolivia is a poor country, it _____ the world's largest lithium reserves.

C Summary

Complete the summary with the appropriate words and expressions.

recall	intelligent	surroundings	mobile
eating	distinguishes	abstract	change

A chameleon is a lizard notable for its ability to _____ colors. This ability is not the only thing that _____ chameleons from other lizards: they also have independently _____ eyes, and unique tongues that allow them to catch prey. Some chameleons change colors in order to blend in with their _____. Others do so as a signal of their physiological state.

Elephants are highly _____ animals with truly remarkable memories. The average elephant spends much of its day _____ and finding food. In fact, its memory may reach as far back as 30 years to _____ a place where it ate in the past. In addition to these mental abilities, elephants can paint _____ pictures, and some of these have been sold at auctions for a great deal of money.

TRANSPORTATION OLD AND NEW

Streetcars

Pre-reading Activity

True or False?

1. T – F: In the U.S.A., streetcars are only operated to attract tourists.
2. T – F: A streetcar gets its power from an overhead wire.
3. T – F: A streetcar runs on rails and is powered by electricity.

Today, buses are the most common form of transportation in many cities. Have you ever thought about how that happened? From the late 1800s until the 1940s, streetcars were more widespread than buses. Streetcars are small trains that run along tracks laid in city streets, and their power source is a network of overhead electric wires. Every large American city used to be crisscrossed by streetcar lines.

Between 1936 and 1950, a company called National City Lines began buying all the streetcar companies. National City Lines was set up by a number of businesses such as Standard Oil of California, General Motors, and Firestone Tire that would profit from replacing streetcars with buses. (1) Then National City Lines had an excuse for shutting them down. (2)

(3) This happened in 45 American cities, including Phoenix, Detroit, New York City, and Baltimore. (4) Although a lawsuit in 1947 revealed the <u>conspiracy</u>, it was too late to restore the dismantled streetcar lines. (5) Moreover, the companies backing National City Lines were making a lot of money from buses.

Fortunately, city leaders are now reversing this trend. A few cities, like San Francisco and Boston, kept their streetcars in service and are adding new lines now. Others, like Los Angeles, are restoring tracks to the routes where the streetcars used to run. Streetcars offer a number of transportation advantages: they are electric, so they do not pollute our cities, and they offer a smooth, quiet ride. Some people may wonder why cities are bringing back an old-fashioned mode of transportation. Perhaps streetcars were a good idea the first time and should never have been replaced.

Reading Tips

usage of "back"

verb

1. to support a person, thing, or plan, making them more like to succeed

   I backed him financially.

2. to move backwards

   She backed her car into the garage.

adverb

1. in the opposite direction that is behind you

   Don't look back! There's a strange man following us.

2. used for talking about a period of time in the past

   Back in the early 90's, 'New Kids On The Block' were very popular.

1   **What is the main idea of the passage?**

    a. advocating for the return of streetcars

    b. discussing public transportation in U.S. cities

    c. suggesting that buses are superior to streetcars

    d. discussing the history and benefits of streetcars

    e. explaining the rise of buses in public transportation

2   **Which is closest in meaning to the word "conspiracy"?**

    a. plot

    b. reason

    c. excuse

    d. answer

    e. presence

3   **Which of the following is NOT true?**

    a. A streetcar is a small electric train.

    b. In modern cities, streetcars are still operating.

    c. The first streetcars were installed in the 1900s.

    d. Buses were common in American cities after 1940.

    e. In the 1920s, many large-sized U.S. cities had streetcar lines.

4   **Why did National City Lines buy up all the streetcar systems?**

    a. to change the way cities developed

    b. to replace them with subway systems

    c. to encourage people to use public transit

    d. to close them down and earn money from running buses

    e. to increase their efficiency by managing many at the same time

5   **Where does the following sentence best fit in the passage?**

> They gradually reduced service on the streetcar routes to make them less popular, and then, as people stopped riding them, they became unprofitable.

    a. (1)   b. (2)   c. (3)   d. (4)   e. (5)

The Space Elevator

Pre-reading Activity

Look at the title of the passage, and write down five words you think will be in the passage.

_____ _____ _____ _____ _____

Now scan the passage, and see if you were right. How many? _____

One of the world's leading astrophysicists, Bryan Laubscher, is developing   1
an invention called the Mars Elevator. To visualize this, you may want to imagine
the story of _Jack and the Beanstalk_. This is the story of a boy who grew a
beanstalk that reached the heavens. Jack climbed the stalk and entered another
world. The space elevator is similar but of course much more high-tech and better   5
yet, it is real!

Astrophysicists are designing a steel-like ribbon or cable that will be
attached to a platform in the ocean. This cable is designed to be pulled up into
space, where it will then be attached to a space station. People will be able to
travel up and down this elevator by the year 2020. There will be a number of   10
space elevators so that both tourists and businesses can travel into space. To get
there, the average space tourist would simply travel to the nearest ocean elevator
entrance. The trip up into space will take about a week. When they arrive, the
space tourists will be inside a space station and will be able to stay there. There
are other options, too. Astronomers think it will be easy to travel from the space   15
station to the moon, where space tourists can stay in a moon hotel—which is
currently being designed.

The future looks bright for potential space tourists like yourself. It also
looks bright for industry and scientists. Mining companies will travel to space to
mine elements that are scarce on earth.   20
Energy scientists will travel to space
to launch space solar panels that will
<u>orbit</u> the earth. The solar panels will
collect an enormous amount of energy
from the sun and shoot it back to earth   25
where we can use it to heat our homes
and fulfill our energy needs.

Reading Tips

usage of "so that"

1. in order to make something
   happen
   I lowered my voice so (that) Cathy
   couldn't hear.

2. used to say that something
   happens as a result of the
   situation you have just
   mentioned
   There are no buses and taxis so (that)
   we'll have to walk.

Answers p 18

1 **What is the passage mainly about?**

a. encouraging space tourism

b. providing an astronomy lesson

c. explaining how to build a space elevator

d. introducing the concept of a space elevator

e. advocating for governments to build space elevators

2 **Which is closest in meaning to the word "orbit"?**

a. light

b. follow

c. realize

d. observe

e. revolve

3 **What is the author's attitude toward space elevators?**

a. neutral

b. dubious

c. skeptical

d. optimistic

e. questioning

4 **Why does the author mention "*Jack and the Beanstalk*"?**

a. to imply that space elevators are fictional

b. to suggest what the space elevator would look like

c. to explain what the building materials would include

d. to suggest that children would enjoy space elevator trips

e. to imply that the idea of space elevators came from this story

5 **Where can the space tourists stay when they travel up into space?**

A Words

A1. Fill in the blank according to the definition.

dismantle	widespread	unprofitable	reverse	fulfill

1 _____: common; found in many places

2 _____: being without monetary reward; having no advantages

3 _____: to separate something into its different parts; to demolish it

4 _____: to finish something; to satisfy someone's need, demand, etc.

5 _____: to move backwards; to change one's opinion to the opposite one

A2. Choose the most appropriate word for each blank.

1 I thought that his _____ for being late was not reasonable.
   a. conceal   b. excuse   c. imagination   d. fulfillment

2 My rice cooker has an automatic _____, so it does all the work for me.
   a. connection   b. recovery   c. temperature   d. mode

3 There is a _____ on the roof of our house to make electricity and hot water.
   a. microwave   b. transformer   c. Martian   d. solar panel

4 Although she wears secondhand, _____ clothes, she looks beautiful in all of them.
   a. modern   b. old-fashioned   c. lovely   d. dandy

5 Fresh water is a _____ resource in most of Australia since the biggest part of this country is desert.
   a. contaminated   b. lukewarm   c. scarce   d. viable

A3. Complete each sentence with one of the words from the box.

conspiracy	smooth	high-tech	orbit	route

1 Seattle and San Jose are centers of the _____ industry.

2 Linda's new silk bed sheets were very _____ and comfortable.

3 The new bus _____ passes quite close to my apartment building.

4 Sometimes Pluto's _____ brings it closer to the Sun than Neptune.

5 When a political leader is killed, people always suspect a(n) _____.

B Expressions and Phrases

B1. Fill in the blank using an expression from the box.

up and down	both A and B	from A to B	fortunately

1 _____, it stopped raining, so we will enjoy our day at the beach.

2 Roller coasters go _____ so quickly that I always get motion sickness.

3 The train will take us _____ New York _____ Boston in two hours.

4 _____ cheating _____ lying could cause a student to be expelled from school.

B2. Complete each sentence with an expression from the reading passages.
(Change the form of the verb if necessary.)

bring back	shut down	set up	be attached to

1 We need an advisor to help _____ business in Japan.

2 The evil scientist's invention will _____ the dead as zombies!

3 A price tag _____ each article, so you can check the price for yourself.

4 Some colleges in the region _____ due to the decreasing number of students last year.

C Summary

Complete the summary with the appropriate words and expressions.

attached	electric	travel	transportation
profits	recognized	economical	cable

Streetcars are _____ trains that operate via power from overhead wires, and they used to be the common form of _____ in U.S. cities. In the 1940s, National City Lines began buying the streetcar systems to close them down. This company was made up of corporations that would earn large _____ by building and running buses. Today, that mistake has been _____, and streetcars are returning to American cities.

A space elevator is a very long _____ anchored to the Earth somewhere near the equator. The other end will be high up in space, _____ to a space station. People will be able to _____ up and down the cable, although the trip will take about a week. This will make trips further into space much easier and more _____.

BREAKING BARRIERS

Barriers Broken in Tiny Tuva

Pre-reading Activity

Write down the names of female politicians.

_____

Write down the name of the woman who served as Prime Minister in Great Britain from 1979 to 1990.

_____

Breaking down social barriers is important as people strive to help the world become more equal. Today, many countries have female presidents or prime ministers, but you may not have heard of Khertek Anchimaa-Toka. She was the first non-royal woman to become a head of state. She was born in 1912 to an extremely poor peasant family in Tuva, an <u>autonomous</u> republic in what is now south central Russia, near Mongolia. Although both of her parents were illiterate, Khertek taught herself to both read and write. She spoke Mongolian as her first language and quickly learned to speak Russian fluently. She went to university on a scholarship from the Soviet government, becoming one of only a few people in Tuva to graduate from college.

When she returned home, her education enabled her to become a powerful figure in the local government. What's more, the USSR's central government in Moscow rewarded her for her achievements by promoting her higher and higher within Tuva's regional government. By 1940, when she was 28 years old, she was appointed as the head of Tuva's government, the first woman to hold that position. The Tuvan people were surprisingly comfortable with a woman in politics. During World War II, she worked to gather materials, like rubber and metal, to help the Soviet army fight against Nazi Germany. After the war, she spent most of her time working for social progress and fighting against poverty.

Khertek died in November of 2008 at age 96. She lived long enough to see women, like Margaret Thatcher in Great Britain and Angela Merkel in Germany, become leaders of their countries. Although she is now a(n)

_____ person in Tuva because of her work in the Communist Party, many people celebrate her as a great example of a woman who rose above her circumstances and succeeded.

1

5

10

15

20

25

Reading Tips

Tuva is a federal subject of Russia. It is located in the very center of Asia and has a population of over three hundred thousand people.

Russia is officially called the Russia Federation. It comprises eighty three federal subjects.

The USSR stands for the Union of Soviet Socialist Republics, in short the Soviet Union. It existed in Eurasia from 1922 to 1991.

1 **What is the main idea of the passage?**

   a. discussing the history of the Tuva Republic

   b. discussing the leadership style of Khertek Anchimaa-Toka

   c. comparing Khertek Anchimaa-Toka with other Soviet leaders

   d. discussing the life and achievements of Khertek Anchimaa-Toka

   e. comparing Khertek Anchimaa-Toka with other female world leaders

2 **Which is closest in meaning to the word "autonomous"?**

   a. poor

   b. social

   c. wealthy

   d. dependent

   e. independent

3 **What can be inferred from the passage?**

   a. Khertek Anchimaa-Toka was not an effective leader.

   b. Khertek Anchimaa-Toka taught her parents to read and write.

   c. Khertek Anchimaa-Toka introduced important reforms in Tuva.

   d. Khertek Anchimaa-Toka is not well-known outside of Tuva and Russia.

   e. Khertek Anchimaa-Toka became leader of Tuva because she was a woman.

4 **Which best fits in the blank?**

   a. controversial

   b. successful

   c. valueless

   d. oblivious

   e. famous

5 **How did Khertek Anchimaa-Toka aid the Soviet Union during the Second World War?**

Breaking the Glass Ceiling in India

Pre-reading Activity

What do you think?

Agree - Disagree	Men and women have equal rights.
Agree - Disagree	Women are better in leadership roles than men.
Agree - Disagree	Men are better at science and math than women.
Agree - Disagree	Men and women should earn the same money for the same job.

The term *glass ceiling* refers to the idea that women and members of certain other groups can climb to a certain point in their jobs, but no higher. Fortunately, one of the world's greatest women, Indira Gandhi, decided not to accept the status quo based on her gender. You've probably heard of Mohandas Gandhi, the man who helped India peacefully win independence from Great Britain. Although Indira Gandhi was not related to Mohandas Gandhi, they were very similar in political ideology. She also advocated for independence, and she did so by focusing on peaceful methods rather than violence.

Indira Gandhi came from one of India's most powerful families, and her father was India's first prime minister. When she was just nine years old, she was already helping her father in his struggle against British colonial rule. One time, as the Gandhi's family home was under British police surveillance, she helped sneak important documents out of the house in her school bag! When she was older, she went to Oxford University in England on a scholarship, and after her graduation she became active in Indian politics. She served as both president of the Indian National Congress and Minister of Information and Broadcasting. It was unprecedented for a woman to hold such political positions in conservative India. In 1966, at the age of 49 years, she was elected prime minister of India, the first and to date only woman ever to hold that position.

Gandhi's main challenge was to bring unity to her country. Sadly, this struggle cost Indira her life: in 1984, two of her Sikh bodyguards, unhappy with the struggle of the Sikh ethnic community in India, assassinated her. Today, she is considered a hero, not just in India but around the world. In one <u>international survey</u>, she was easily voted the greatest woman of the past 1,000 years!

1

5

10

15

20

25

Reading Tips

usage of "that"

determiner: used to refer to someone or something that has already been mentioned
Could you give me that book?

relative pronoun: used to introduce a relative clause
I lost the watch that you bought me for my birthday.

conjunction: used to connect two clauses and introduce a fact, idea, statement, reason, etc.
• I'm sure that you'll be okay by yourself.
• She has never told the fact that she already met him.

1 **What is the best alternative title of the passage?**

a. India's Greatest Leader
b. The Death of Indira Gandhi
c. India's First Female Prime Minister
d. A History of Assassinations in India
e. The Gandhis: India's Political Dynasty

2 **What is true about Indira Gandhi's father?**

a. He died later than his daughter did.
b. He was a spy for the British government.
c. He served as prime minister before she did.
d. He snuck documents out of the house for the British.
e. He held several important positions in the Indian government.

3 **What is the author's attitude toward Indira Gandhi?**

a. neutral
b. sarcastic
c. admiring
d. indifferent
e. pessimistic

4 **Which best fits in the blanks?**

> Indira Gandhi might have _____ many more great things if she had not been _____ .

a. failed, assassinated
b. achieved, dethroned
c. known about, elected
d. accomplished, murdered
e. been remembered for, female

5 **What can be inferred from the international survey?**

a. Most surveys are worthless and inaccurate.
b. Indira Gandhi's assassination made her famous.
c. Female leaders do not usually attract much attention.
d. Indira Gandhi's achievements were highly significant.
e. Many people have already forgotten about Indira Gandhi.

A Words

A1. Fill in the blank according to the definition.

republic	gender	elect	barrier	strive

1 _____ : the fact of being male or female
2 _____ : to try continuously with great effort
3 _____ : obstacle; something that gets in the way
4 _____ : a country ruled by representatives that people elect
5 _____ : to choose someone to be a representative by voting

A2. Choose the most appropriate word for each blank.

1 Countries like the USA and Canada are home to people from many _____ groups.
  a. independent   b. citizenship   c. racing   d. ethnic

2 Some countries _____ for many years to achieve their independence.
  a. identify   b. struggle   c. debate   d. conceive

3 In Singapore and Hong Kong, there are still many wonderful old _____ buildings built during the British rule.
  a. colonial   b. ruined   c. elevated   d. modern

4 He's very intelligent, and he went to Cambridge on a(n) _____.
  a. insurance   b. election   c. scholarship   d. insistence

5 As elementary school education is not compulsory in Cambodia, many people there are _____.
  a. dyslexic   b. tycoons   c. industrialists   d. illiterate

A3. Complete each sentence with one of the words from the box.

appoint	progress	controversial	unprecedented	unity

1 There has been no _____ on updating our computer system.
2 The movie was very _____ because of all the violence it showed.
3 I wonder who the president will _____ to the Supreme Court next.
4 A(n) _____ amount of rain fell in Taiwan after the recent typhoon.
5 Both political parties showed surprising _____ when they drafted the new law.

B Expressions and Phrases

B1. Fill in the blank using an expression in the box.

to date	to a certain point	what's more	under surveillance

1 I can tolerate hot stuffy rooms only up _____, and then I need air.

2 _____, donations to the charity have exceeded one million dollars.

3 The doctor says I have to stay home. _____, I can't exercise for two weeks!

4 After 9/11, the U.S. government angered many by keeping its own citizens _____

_____.

B2. Complete each sentence with an expression from the reading passages. (Change the form of the verb if necessary.)

focus on	fight against	rise above	teach oneself

1 James finally _____ all the troubles at his new school.

2 Please stop playing games and _____ your assignment.

3 She _____ to read, speak, and write Chinese when she was younger.

4 People protested in the streets to _____ the new Free Trade Agreement.

C Summary

Complete the summary with the appropriate words and expressions.

positions	such as	assassinated	first
political	education	leader	achievements

Khertek Anchimaa-Toka was the _____ person not from a royal family to become a head of government. Because of her _____, she rose quickly in the government of Tuva and became the republic's _____. This happened many years before recent world leaders _____ Angela Merkel and Margaret Thatcher took power.

Indira Gandhi was born into a powerful _____ family in India. Her father was India's first prime minister. She had several high _____ in India's government before becoming prime minister in 1966. Unfortunately, she was _____ by her bodyguards in 1984, but her _____ have won her respect all over the world.

GREAT WORKS OF LITERATURE

The Lord of the Rings

Pre-reading Activity

What is your favorite book of all time?

What genre is it?

love story ___ adventure ___ science fiction ___ thriller ___ historical novel ___

Who was the author of *The Lord of the Rings*?

Peter Jackson   J.R.R. Tolkien   J.K. Rowling

Many people became familiar with the epic story *The Lord of the Rings* 1
because of the three films directed by Peter Jackson. Released to theaters between
2001 and 2003, the films were seen and loved by audiences all over the world. As
a result of the trilogy's success, there has been a renewed interest in the original
books by J.R.R. Tolkien. 5

Tolkien had originally planned *The Lord of the Rings* as a sequel to his
earlier novel *The Hobbit*. Because that book had been so popular, his publisher
wanted him to continue the story. Tolkien, a professor of linguistics at university,
warned <u>him</u> that he was a slow writer, but no one expected that he would need
12 years to finish *LOTR*! What's more, the book took another six years to be 10
published, because there were several difficulties to overcome.

Tolkien had trouble deciding how to begin the story. Although he made
several attempts, the plot and the characters would not <u>resolve</u> themselves in his
mind. He didn't have the ideas he needed, and it took him another two years to
decide what direction he wanted to take. Moreover, he had to stop writing for a 15
period of time during the early 1940s because he was too busy teaching. In 1949,
he finally finished writing it.

LOTR was written as a single book, but at the time of its publication in the
early 1950s, Britain was still recovering from <u>World War II</u>. Many important
things were in short supply, including paper. Because 20
of the paper shortage, Tolkien's publisher decided
to split *LOTR* into three separate books. Since then,
the three volumes have been translated into about
40 languages and have sold millions of copies
worldwide. What began as a fanciful children's 25
story is now seen as a major work of 20th-century
literature.

Reading Tips

usage of "including"

preposition: used for mentioning
someone or something is part of a
larger group or amount

He has many pets, including two
hamsters.

1   **What is the main idea of the passage?**

a. giving a biography of J.R.R. Tolkien

b. introducing readers to *The Hobbit*

c. explaining the plot of *The Lord of the Rings*

d. describing the publishing history of *The Lord of the Rings*

e. explaining why *The Lord of the Rings* was published as three books

2   **What does the word "him" refer to?**

a. J.R.R. Tolkien

b. his co-writer

c. his publisher

d. his colleague

e. Peter Jackson

3   **Which is closest in meaning to the word "resolve"?**

a. follow

b. clarify

c. finish

d. leave

e. write

4   **Which of the following is NOT mentioned?**

a. Tolkien taught linguistics at university.

b. It took Tolkien 12 years to write *LOTR*.

c. For a while, Tolkien was too busy to write.

d. *The Hobbit* had been a very successful book.

e. The publisher pushed Tolkien to write *LOTR* in a hurry.

5   **Why does the author mention "World War II"?**

a. because Tolkien was German

b. to suggest that Tolkien fought in the war

c. to imply that Tolkien was killed in the war

d. to give an idea how serious the shortages were

e. because the original *LOTR* manuscript was destroyed in the war

Don Quixote

Pre-reading Activity

Read the trivia questions and circle what you think is the answer.

1. What country is *Don Quixote* set in?   Spain   Mexico
2. What does Don Quixote believe he is?   king   knight
3. What time period was *Don Quixote* set?   1700s   1600s
4. What is Don Quixote's companion named?   Dulcinea   Sancho

The story of Cervantes's *Don Quixote* is perhaps the most famous work ¹ of Spanish literature. When it was written, it was so popular that it helped establish Spanish as the main language of what is now Spain. Set in the early 1600s, it follows the life of an old man who, after reading too many stories about knights and chivalry, comes to believe he too is a famous knight. He convinces ⁵ himself that a poor farm girl who lives nearby is actually a beautiful lady named Dulcinea. He does not inform her of this, however. He decides to set out in search of adventure, accompanied by his neighbor, Sancho Panza, and their journey around Spain is recounted in a number of episodic stories.

One of Don Quixote's most notable quirks is his tendency to believe that ¹⁰ _____. For example, in Don Quixote's mind, a windmill becomes a giant. For centuries, readers have enjoyed reading about the fantastical exploits of Don Quixote and Sancho. The reader is aware of the reality of the situations, but Don Quixote and Sancho exist in a world of make-believe. It is this incongruence that makes the novel funny, entertaining, yet still ¹⁵ <u>insightful</u>.

Cervantes's story did not become famous only because of the humor. While Don Quixote is a funny character, he is portrayed as a kind-hearted person who acts with great chivalry, which means that he embraces the importance of ²⁰ honesty and bravery. Don Quixote is always kind toward his friends and polite and courteous to everyone he meets, and he has come to be seen as a role model for how people should treat each other. Today, Don Quixote is not viewed entirely as a comic character, ²⁵ but a dreamer who knows what is truly important in life.

Reading Tips

too + adjective + to + verb
= so + adjective + that + subject
 + can't / couldn't + verb
: so much of a particular quality that something is not possible

He is too young to see that movie.

= He is so young that he can't see that movie.

1 **What is paragraph 3 mainly about?**

a. how people treat each other

b. the definition of the chivalry

c. the true meaning of *Don Quixote*

d. the evaluation of Spanish literature

e. the reason Cervantes wrote *Don Quixote*

2 **Which is closest in meaning to the word "insightful"?**

a. viable

b. believable

c. perceptive

d. observable

e. disrespectful

3 **What is true about Dulcinea?**

a. She is exceedingly beautiful.

b. She is in love with Don Quixote.

c. She is not originally from Spain.

d. She does not know that Don Quixote calls her Dulcinea.

e. She goes with Don Quixote and Sancho Panza on their journey.

4 **Which best fits in the blank?**

a. he has to save the world

b. Sancho Panza is his servant

c. he is a guardian of Princess Dulcinea

d. everybody looks up to him as a knight

e. normal things and objects are dangerous

5 **What can be inferred from the passage?**

a. Don Quixote was good at geography.

b. Don Quixote had an eye for art and beauty.

c. Don Quixote had no patience with injustice.

d. Don Quixote liked to talk with his neighbors.

e. Don Quixote pretended to be silly to his friends.

A Words

A1. Fill in the blank according to the definition.

direct	release	sequel	quirk	recount

1 _____: a characteristic that is unique or different

2 _____: to tell someone about events that have happened to you

4 _____: a book or movie that continues the story of an earlier one

3 _____: to be in charge of something or control it for a group of people

5 _____: to make a book, film, etc. available to people; to set someone free

A2. Choose the most appropriate word for each blank.

1 In a foreign country, ordering food in restaurants can be a(n) _____!
   a. itinerary   b. sequel   c. adventure   d. preoccupation

2 Children can enter the swimming pool area but only if _____ by their parents.
   a. drowned   b. accompanied   c. submerged   d. washed

3 I enjoy _____ stories of outer space like *Star Wars* and *Star Trek*.
   a. incomplete   b. unknown   c. possible   d. epic

4 Your comments about my story were very _____. Thanks very much for your help.
   a. unsightly   b. illiterate   c. ruinous   d. insightful

5 The original book received a(n) _____ interest after the movie released.
   a. renewed   b. unrelated   c. attached   d. cultivated

A3. Complete each sentence with one of the words from the box.

courteous	shortage	overcome	separate	notable

1 Two _____ governments were officially established in Korea in 1948.

2 It was _____ that Franklin invented so many useful things.

3 Tom had to _____ the disadvantages of his upbringing to be a successful judge.

4 She was always kind and _____ to me, so we easily became the best of friends.

5 It's difficult to take care of patients because of a(n) _____ of medicine in Africa.

B Expressions and Phrases

B1. Fill in the blank using an expression from the box.

in search of	as a result of	in short supply	how to

1 The immigrants came to Australia _____ a better life.

2 Due to the recent economic downturn, jobs were _____.

3 I managed to find out _____ use the digital camera that I bought recently.

4 _____ the economic recession, over one million people have become unemployed.

B2. Complete each sentence with an expression from the reading passages. (Change the form of the verb if necessary.)

be aware of	set out	be translated into	make an attempt

1 We have to _____ before rush hour starts. Hurry up and get ready.

2 *Twilight* _____ more than 30 languages as soon as it was published.

3 Jeremy didn't even _____ to finish the test. I wonder why he did that.

4 _____ you _____ the procedure for registering for classes this semester?

C Summary

Complete the summary with the appropriate words and expressions.

sequel	literature	shortage	role model
knights	release	journey	published

J.R.R. Tolkien's *The Lord of the Rings* attracted new interest after the _____ of the three films by Peter Jackson. *LOTR* was planned as a _____ to Tolkien's earlier book, *The Hobbit*, which had been successful when it was _____. *LOTR* took Tolkien 12 years to write. When it was published, there was a paper _____, so the publisher decided to split it into three separate volumes.

Don Quixote is the most famous work of Spanish _____. It concerns a man who has read too many stories about _____ and has come to believe that he is one. He and his neighbor Sancho Panza set out on a _____ through Spain. Don Quixote's belief in treating people honorably raises him above the level of comedy and makes him a sort of _____.

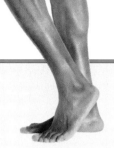

CUBA

Leaving Cuba

Pre-reading Activity

True or False?

1. T – F: Havana is the largest city in Cuba.
2. T – F: Fidel Castro became Prime Minister of Cuba in February 1959.
3. T – F: Cuba is an archipelago of islands located in the Caribbean Sea.

Many different people from many different countries immigrate to the U.S.A. for a variety of reasons. The United States government encourages Cubans to immigrate, not because it holds Cuba in high esteem, but for the opposite reason: the United States considers Cuba an enemy nation. `1`

The United States and Cuba have vastly different political systems. When Fidel Castro became the leader of Cuba, some of his actions angered the United States. Because the United States government thinks that the Cuban people's quality of life is harsh, and the repression they face from their government is unacceptable, the U.S. has set up special rules for those Cubans wishing to immigrate to America. _____ people from other countries have a lengthy, time-consuming application process, people from Cuba are viewed as political refugees. Therefore, they can immigrate to the United States without going through the standard—and very tedious—procedures. `5` `10`

Because of this special policy, many Cubans have flocked to the United States. The Cuban government objects to its citizens <u>forsaking</u> their homeland for foreign shores, and it does its best to make things very difficult for them. Many Cubans build small, rickety boats and rafts and sail from the island of Cuba to the state of Florida. This trip is very dangerous, and many people have died attempting the crossing. In 1973, the United States government made it more difficult for Cubans to enter the U.S. by using <u>this perilous method</u> of crossing the sea. That year, the U.S. government established the "wet foot dry foot" policy. Under that policy, if Cuban immigrants are found at sea, they must return to Cuba. If they are found on land, then they can remain in the United States. `15` `20`

Reading Tips

words related to "migrate"

immigrate: to come to a country to live there
Many people immigrate to the U.S.A.

emigrate: to leave one's country to live in another country
She will emigrate from Japan to Canada.

migrate: birds or animals to travel from one place, country, or region to another for warmer weather at a particular time of the year
The birds migrate to South Africa.

1 What is the main idea of the passage?

a. how to move to the U.S.
b. the dangers of fleeing Cuba
c. immigration to other countries
d. immigrating from Cuba to the U.S.
e. the U.S.-Cuba political relationship

2 Which is closest in meaning to the word "forsaking"?

a. saving
b. serving
c. forgiving
d. deceiving
e. abandoning

3 Which best fits in the blank?

a. Since
b. While
c. However
d. Therefore
e. In addition

4 What does "this perilous method" refer to?

_____

5 When are Cuban refugees returned to Cuba?

_____

The Cuban-American Community of Miami

02

Pre-reading Activity

1. What is the main language used in Cuba?
2. What word means one who can speak two languages?
3. What state in the U.S.A. do you think receives the most Cuban refugees?

Miami has the largest population of Cuban-Americans in the United States. 1
There are many reasons why they choose to live there. First of all, it is very close
to Cuba, so Miami is the point of entry for many Cuban immigrants. __(A)__ ,
there is already a large and well-established Cuban-American community in
Miami, so new arrivals feel comfortable living and working in a city where the 5
inhabitants already know and understand their Cuban culture and history.

One section of Miami is called Little Havana because so many Cuban-
Americans have settled there. Havana is the capital of Cuba, and Little Havana
could be called the capital of the Cuban-American community of Miami. A
multitude of restaurants specialize in Cuban food, and many department stores 10
sell Cuban products. Most schools in this area are bilingual, so students speak
both English and Spanish, the official language of Cuba. Little Havana is also
famous for its film and music festivals that celebrate all aspects of Cuban culture.

The Cuban-Americans of Miami continue to cherish and remember Cuban
cultural traditions. For example, many people play dominoes and chess in the 15
parks of Miami, as they did in Cuba. Bands perform such Cuban musical styles
as *habanera*, *guaracha*, and *danzón*. Cuban-Americans often live in
extended family groups, including grandparents, parents, unmarried
children, and married children. Cuban-Americans have a special
celebration on Christmas Eve, __(B)__ they call Noche Buena. For 20
this fun festival, families get together for the entire day. While a
man in the family keeps busy roasting an entire pig, the children
play, and the elders reminisce about the old days in Cuba and the
good days to come in America. Noche Buena is one gigantic
party. Traditions such as these help the Cuban-Americans 25
maintain and perpetuate their Cuban heritage.

Reading Tips

numerical prefixes

1/2: half-, semi-, demi-
  e.g., half-day, semi-circle, demigod
1: mono-, uni-
  e.g., monolingual, unicorn
2: di-, bi-
  e.g., binocular, carbon dioxide
3: tri- e.g., triangle
4: quadri- e.g., quadrilateral
5: penta- e.g., pentagon
6: hexa- e.g., hexagon

1 **What is the main idea of paragraph 3?**

a. bands playing traditional Cuban music
b. the way Cuban people celebrate Christmas
c. Cuban music's influence on American music
d. relationships between Cuban family members
e. the traditions maintained by Cuban-American in the U.S.

2 **Which is closest in meaning to the word "inhabitants"?**

a. servants
b. refugees
c. residents
d. immigrants
e. descendants

3 **What can be inferred from the passage?**

a. Cubans often return home to visit.
b. Many people in Miami probably speak Spanish.
c. The U.S. and Cuba have a close, friendly relationship.
d. Miami must also be home to many other immigrant groups.
e. Most of the Cuban-Americans probably work for the city of Miami.

4 **What is the type of the passage?**

a. epic
b. narrative
c. persuasive
d. informative
e. argumentative

5 **Which best fits in the blanks?**

	(A)		(B)
a.	On the other hand	...	that
b.	For instance	...	which
c.	As a result	...	that
d.	In addition	...	which
e.	Therefore	...	when

A Words

A1. Fill in the blank according to the definition.

perpetuate	heritage	perilous	establish	policy

1 _____: very dangerous; hazardous

2 _____: to set up or to create an organization, system, etc.

3 _____: to make something such as a process or situation continue to exist

4 _____: traditions and qualities that a country or society has had for many years

5 _____: a set of actions and plans officially implemented by a government, ruler, political party, etc.

A2. Choose the most appropriate word for each blank.

1 Leaving one's _____ must be a painful, emotional experience.

   a. donation   b. portfolio   c. investment   d. homeland

2 My commute is very _____, so it's always late when I get home.

   a. networked   b. time-consuming   c. efficient   d. interconnected

3 If you'd like to become a member, please fill out this _____ form.

   a. application   b. beta testing   c. credit   d. resignation

4 Burma, Iraq, Iran, and several other countries are notorious for political _____.

   a. destruction   b. openness   c. repression   d. stability

5 It is completely _____ to talk on your cell phone during a play or a movie.

   a. unlikely   b. unacceptable   c. elegant   d. unknown

A3. Complete each sentence with one of the words from the box.

harsh	tedious	flock	rickety	arrival

1 Siberia is famous for its long _____ winters.

2 The staircase looks _____, so let's not go upstairs.

3 My history course is so _____ that I fall asleep every day!

4 In countries like Cambodia, beggars _____ to tourists to ask for money.

5 My flight's _____ time is 9 a.m., so I'll be able to attend the lunch meeting.

B Expressions and Phrases

B1. Fill in the blank using an expression in the box.

first of all	for the entire day	such as	a multitude of

1 _____, make sure you have all the ingredients.

2 I could roam around in the markets of Marrakech _____!

3 In New York City, you can meet people from _____ countries.

4 The museum has paintings by impressionist artists _____ Renoir and Monet.

B2. Complete each sentence with an expression from the reading passages. (Change the form of the verb if necessary.)

set up	go through	object to	specialize in

1 My doctor _____ ear, nose, and throat problems.

2 I _____ the idea that all American tourists are loud and rude.

3 When I moved to California, I had a hard time _____ my first bank account.

4 When we arrive, we have to _____ Immigration to get our passports stamped.

C Summary

Complete the summary with the appropriate words and expressions.

settle	refugees	immigration	traditions
repression	commonplace	geographically	shores

The U.S. government disapproves of Cuba's political system and encourages Cubans to flee to safety. Many have left Cuba because of its political _____ and commenced new lives in the U.S.A. For nationals of most countries, U.S. _____ is a long process, but it is streamlined for Cubans. Cuban _____ will only be turned back if they are intercepted before they arrive on U.S. _____.

Miami has the US's largest population of Cuban-Americans, as it is _____ close to Cuba. Many new immigrants _____ there and enjoy a life where Cuban customs and _____ are part of the fabric of society. Cuban products can readily be found in stores, and Cuban music and other forms of entertainment are _____. Cuban holidays are also commonly observed in Miami.

EXTRAORDINARY ABILITIES

Night Vision

Pre-reading Activity

True or False?

1. T – F: Rats have eyeshine that is the color white.
2. T – F: Animals can see even in complete darkness.
3. T – F: Different animals have different colors of eyeshine.

Have you ever wished you could see in the dark as well as an animal? In action movies, we often see characters wearing special goggles that reveal things not visible in darkness. Everything looks green, but we can see the shapes and outlines clearly. As a matter of fact, this is somewhat similar to the way animals' night vision works.

You may have noticed eyeshine in pictures of animals, or seen it for yourself when light hits an animal's eyes. Dogs, cats, and many other animals have an iridescent layer of tissue called the *tapetum lucidum* either behind or inside the retina of each eye. The purpose of this tissue is to reflect light deeper into the eye. For many species, it contributes to their excellent night vision, and it helps them hunt prey.

Different species have different colors of eyeshine. The light reflecting back from the eyes of dogs, cats, and raccoons tends to be yellow. Rats, other rodents, and birds usually have eyes that shine red. Other animals' eyes may reflect white, yellow, green, or pink light. In each case, the color is related to the type of cells that make up the *tapetum lucidum*, as well as the chemicals inside the cells.

Eyeshine has the function of <u>augmenting</u> animals' night vision, but humans have found other uses for it. ___(A)___, when people are searching for certain types of animals, their eyeshine may be helpful in identifying them. Also, eyeshine inspired humans to invent substances that reflect light at night. Strips containing this substance are used to alert us to safety hazards such as raised sections of pavement. ___(B)___ humans cannot see so well at night, we have still found ways to benefit from this fascinating animal trait.

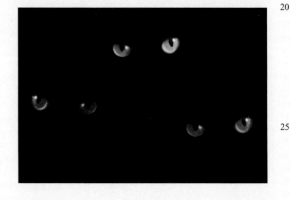

Reading Tips

subject-verb agreement

either A or B

Either you or <u>he</u> <u>is</u> going with me.

both A and B

<u>Both she and her sister</u> <u>are</u> able to stay with us.

neither A nor B

Neither my parents nor <u>my brother</u> <u>is</u> at home.

not only A but also B

Not only the students but also <u>their teacher</u> <u>was</u> in the classroom.

B as well as A

<u>All of the grandchildren</u> as well as Ron <u>want</u> to visit their grandparents.

1   What is the main idea of the passage?

    a. humans' night vision

    b. eyeshine and its benefits

    c. how animals see in the dark

    d. animals' eyeshine in the dark

    e. different colors of eyes in the animal world

2   Which is closest in meaning to the word "augmenting"?

    a. subtracting

    b. increasing

    c. degrading

    d. debating

    e. arguing

3   Which best fits in the blanks?

(A)		(B)
a. However	⋯	In fact
b. For instance	⋯	When
c. Furthermore	⋯	Instead
d. As a result	⋯	Consequently
e. For example	⋯	Even though

4   Which of the following is true?

    a. People have applied animals' night vision to practical uses.

    b. Night vision goggles were originally invented for military use.

    c. Different colors of animals' eyeshine are due to different colors of light.

    d. When you wear the night vision goggles, everything looks somewhat unclear.

    e. When you wear the night vision goggles during the day, it can hurt your eyes.

5   How does the *tapetum lucidum* aid animals' night vision?

    a. It reflects light back into the eye.

    b. It makes everything appear green.

    c. It glows in the dark and produces light.

    d. It enables the animal to see colors at night.

    e. It reflects light outward, away from the animal.

Extrasensory Perception

Pre-reading Activity

What do you think?

Agree - Disagree   Some people have special abilities outside of the five main senses.
Agree - Disagree   Some people can see the future or predict the future.
Agree - Disagree   Some people can see people who have passed away.

The idea of extrasensory perception, or ESP has existed in many human cultures all throughout recorded history. ESP refers to a group of abilities that lie outside the five senses. It may be used to gather information, to see objects located far away, or to control certain aspects of the environment. Although ESP has been the subject of scientific investigation at universities and by governments around the world, there seems to be little hard data to confirm its existence. _____, many people believe that these abilities exist.

One of the first major studies of ESP took place at Duke University in North Carolina in the 1930s. J.B. Rhine, who invented the term *parapsychology* as a more scientific way of talking about ESP, was the first to apply the principles of scientific analysis to this area of study. He used Zener cards, a simple series of 25 cards. Each card would contain one of five symbols: a circle, a square, wavy lines, a cross, or a star. There were five cards with each symbol. "Receiver" subjects in his experiments had to guess which card a "sender" was holding. The results of Rhine's tests suggested that some sort of ESP might have been used, because the "receivers" guessed correctly more often than <u>statistics</u> said they could have. However, other researchers have not been able to <u>replicate</u> his findings exactly.

Since then, many studies have actually yielded similar results: they tend to show only a slight chance that ESP is real, rather than the sort of superhero abilities seen on TV. Still, some people believe that these data are proof enough. Others believe that the evidence needs to be even stronger. Whether or not this debate is ever settled, we can be certain that people will always be fascinated with ESP.

1
5
10
15
20
25

Reading Tips

usage of "used to"

used to + verb: It happened regularly in the past, but it does not happen now.
I used to swim, but I don't have time for it now.

be [get / accustomed] + used to + -ing: It no longer seems strange or difficult.
I'm used to getting up at five in the morning.

be used to + verb: It is used to do something as a means.
Blocks were used to build the house.

1   What is the main idea of paragraph 2?

   a. unusual research methods
   b. how to play with Zener cards
   c. Rhine's experiments with ESP
   d. the reason studies with ESP failed
   e. J.B. Rhine: an inventor of parapsychology

2   Which is closest in meaning to the word "replicate"?

   a. stop
   b. copy
   c. produce
   d. consider
   e. initialize

3   Which best fits in the blank?

   a. Similarly
   b. Therefore
   c. In addition
   d. Regardless
   e. For example

4   What is the author's attitude toward ESP research?

   a. neutral
   b. dubious
   c. skeptical
   d. optimistic
   e. pessimistic

5   Why does the author mention "statistics"?

   a. to imply that ESP is all fake
   b. to imply that ESP is study of statistics
   c. to explain how the card game was conducted
   d. to suggest that people were not really using ESP
   e. to suggest that scientific research methods were used

A Words

A1. Fill in the blank according to the definition.

goggles	reveal	visible	outline	somewhat

1 _____: possible to see

2 _____: more than a little but not too much

3 _____: to show something that was hidden

4 _____: special glasses that protect your eyes

5 _____: a line that shows the edge or shape of something

A2. Choose the most appropriate word for each blank.

1 The police conducted a(n) _____ and concluded that the man was innocent.
   a. panel   b. investigation   c. questionnaire   d. telethon

2 Scientists have discovered a new _____ that kills most cancer cells.
   a. talent   b. eraser   c. physics   d. chemical

3 I _____ my salary by working at a part-time job.
   a. heighten   b. lessen   c. augment   d. decrease

4 The police _____ information relevant to the armed robbery that occurred Monday.
   a. regarded   b. gathered   c. seemed   d. cost

5 There is no _____ yet that life exists on other planets.
   a. principle   b. proof   c. term   d. effect

A3. Complete each sentence with one of the words from the box.

reflects	tissue	debate	principles	confirm

1 When sunlight _____ off the water, it sparkles.

2 It takes a long time for _____ to heal after a burn.

3 Watching politicians _____ is boring, and I always fall asleep.

4 People have understood basic mathematical _____ for centuries.

5 Tomorrow I will call the travel agent to _____ our vacation plans.

B Expressions and Phrases

B1. Fill in the blank using an expression from the box.

| rather than | as a matter of fact | even though | whether or not |

1 _____ it rains, it's still smart to have an umbrella.

2 _____ I couldn't get the perfect score, I passed the test.

3 Actually, I just want to pursue a good reputation _____ fortune.

4 I knew her when we were in middle school. _____, we were in the same class.

**B2. Complete each sentence with an expression from the reading passages.
(Change the form of the verb if necessary.)**

| benefit from | refer to | be fascinated with | take place |

1 We _____ the stories of his childhood in South America.

2 Though he didn't say any names, everyone knew who he was _____.

3 The next meeting is scheduled to _____ in the city of Tokyo, Japan.

4 Many patients will _____ this new medicine created by our medical organization.

C Summary

Complete the summary with the appropriate words and expressions.

| existence | conducted | inspired | reflecting |
| solid | thanks to | depending on | beyond |

Animals possess the ability to see well at night _____ their eyeshine, which is caused by light _____ off the *tapetum lucidum* in the back of the eye. This light may vary in color _____ the species of the animal. Enhanced vision helps them hunt prey in the dark, and it has also _____ humans to develop luminescent materials for use at night.

ESP refers to a group of abilities that exist _____ the five senses. It may be used to gather information that the person wouldn't be able to know via any other means, or to control objects in the environment. Some research has been _____, attempting to prove or disprove the _____ of ESP, but no _____ conclusions have been reached. In the meantime, it is a topic many people are fascinated with.

SKYSCRAPERS

Empire State Building

Pre-reading Activity

How many stories do you think the Empire State Building has?

Which skyscraper would you most like to visit?

The Empire State Building is an iconic emblem of New York City. For many 1
years, it was the tallest building in the city. The World Trade Center's famous
twin towers were much taller, but their destruction in the terrorist attacks of 9/11
returned the Empire State Building to the top position in the Manhattan skyline.
The Empire State Building was not always such a success, however. 5

At the dramatic opening ceremony in 1931, President Herbert Hoover
pushed a button in Washington, D.C., to turn on the building's electricity.
Unfortunately, this happened at the beginning of the Great Depression. At that
time, few businesses were interested in occupying the new building; they couldn't
afford the rent. This meant that the building stood mostly vacant for a long time, 10
earning it the nickname Empty State Building. The rooftop observation deck
_____ to be as profitable as renting offices. Further complicating matters, the
building site was a little too far from public transportation to be convenient.

On top of the Empire State Building, there is a very distinctive spire,
making it quite different from any other building in the area. This was meant as 15
a docking station for dirigibles or zeppelins. In the 1930s, they were becoming
popular as a means of transportation. The top floors of the Empire State Building
were designed to be something like an airport. Strong winds at that height made
docking extremely unsafe, so the idea was abandoned.

Fortunately, as New York grew into the center of the U.S. business and 20
finance sectors, the demand for Manhattan office space increased. Today, the
Empire State Building is the much-loved jewel in the crown of the New York City
skyline.

Reading Tips

such: used to emphasize a quality
in someone or something
such + a(n) + adjective + noun
She is such a generous person.

so: used to emphasize a quality,
amount, feeling
so + adjective (+ a + noun)
She is so generous.

1   What is the main idea of the passage?

   a. explaining how Manhattan was developed
   b. giving a history of skyscrapers in New York
   c. giving a history of the Empire State Building
   d. explaining the history of the word skyscrapers
   e. comparing the Empire State Building to other major skyscrapers

2   Which best fits in the blank?

   a. turned in
   b. turned on
   c. turned up
   d. turned out
   e. turned over

3   Which of the following is NOT true?

   a. The Empire State Building was used as a docking station.
   b. The Empire State Building is currently New York's tallest skyscraper.
   c. The Empire State Building was nicknamed the Empty State Building.
   d. The World Trade Center's Twin Towers were New York's tallest buildings.
   e. The Great Depression affected the occupancy rate of the Empire State Building.

4   What can be inferred from the passage?

   a. Zeppelins have become a popular means of transportation.
   b. The Empire State Building's developers went bankrupt after finishing it.
   c. Many buildings were constructed to resemble the Empire State Building.
   d. The Empire State Building will always be the tallest skyscraper in New York.
   e. When the Empire State Building was planned, people knew less about wind patterns in New York City.

5   What does "This" refer to?

   _____

Petronas Twin Towers

Pre-reading Activity

What do you think?

Agree - Disagree   Having the tallest building is a sign of an advanced country.
Agree - Disagree   Skyscrapers are good for a city's tourism and economy.
Agree - Disagree   Building skyscrapers wastes money and resources.

The Petronas Twin Towers in Malaysia's original capital city, Kuala Lumpur, were the tallest buildings in the world. Construction was completed in 1998, and for the next six years, until Taipei 101 opened, they also had the honor of being the world's tallest buildings.

The towers, which were designed by the architect César Pelli, are unusual in that they are built of reinforced concrete, not steel. The cost of importing steel was too high to be <u>practical</u>. Concrete gives another advantage, too: concrete buildings sway less than those made of steel. The buildings' enormous weight, coupled with the depth of the bedrock below that part of Kuala Lumpur, meant that a very deep—the world's deepest, at 120 meters—foundation was needed.

The Twin Towers were meant to be the showpiece of a development program for Malaysia. Tower One is used by Petronas, the national petroleum company. The second tower is used as commercial office space, with such corporate tenants as Reuters, IBM, Al Jazeera, and Boeing. At the base of the towers, there is an upscale, six-story shopping mall called Suria KLCC, for Kuala Lumpur City Center. It is surrounded by a 17-acre park. Underneath, there is a station on one of Kuala Lumpur's new subway lines.

Visitors may go as high as the skybridge that connects the two towers at the 41st and 42nd floors. This is the world's highest two-story bridge. Only people who work for Petronas or one of the companies in Tower 2 are permitted to go to the higher floors. What's more, only 1,700 people per day are given permits to visit the skybridge. They are given out on a first-come-first-serve basis. If you want to see the view from one of the world's most architecturally important buildings, _____!

Reading Tips

weights and measures

1 acre = 4047 square meters (m^2)
1 yard (yd) = 0.91 meters (m)
1 inch (in) = 2.54 centimeters (cm)
1 foot (ft) = 12 in ≒ 30 cm
1 pound (lb) = 0.454 kilograms (kg)
1 ounce (oz) = 28.35 grams (g)

1   **What is the best alternative title of the passage?**

a. Taipei 101

b. The World's Tallest Buildings

c. Kuala Lumpur's Twin Landmarks

d. The Miracle of Concrete Construction

e. The Companies in Petronas Twin Towers

2   **Which is closest in meaning to the word "practical"?**

a. useful

b. qualified

c. impossible

d. professional

e. sophisticated

3   **Which best fits in the blank?**

a. make a reservation on the Internet

b. show your identity card as you go in

c. get a job at companies in the twin towers

d. make a large donation to the twin towers

e. plan on getting there early in the morning

4   **Which best fits in the blanks?**

> The Petronas Twin Towers were the tallest buildings in the world _____ Taipei 101 _____ them.

a. while, built   b. by, created

c. for, surrendered   d. until, surpassed

e. during, transformed

5   **What is the purpose of the passage?**

a. to explain the benefits of concrete construction

b. to talk about the development of Kuala Lumpur

c. to give an overview of the Petronas Twin Towers

d. to introduce readers to Malaysian building methods

e. to compare the Petronas Twin Towers and Taipei 101

A Words

A1. Fill in the blank according to the definition.

occupy	abandoned	construction	tenant	enormous

1 _____: no longer used

2 _____: to live in or use a place

3 _____: very large in size or in amount

4 _____: a person who rents a residence or business space

5 _____: the process of building things such as a bridge, road, or house

A2. Choose the most appropriate word for each blank.

1 Manhattan is a very _____ district, which lots of wealthy people live in.
   a. sparse   b. dense   c. upscale   d. impoverished

2 The river completely _____ the castle, so no one can go out without a boat.
   a. surrounds   b. attacks   c. excludes   d. undermines

3 The hunter was arrested for using government land without the right _____.
   a. selection   b. time   c. salary   d. permit

4 Chicago is often called America's most _____ interesting city because it is
   the birthplace of the skyscraper.
   a. logistically   b. basically   c. architecturally   d. marginally

5 The Eiffel Tower is perhaps the most famous _____ of Paris.
   a. situation   b. emblem   c. leader   d. fashion

A3. Complete each sentence with one of the words from the box.

afford	vacant	convenient	distinctive	complete

1 Can you really _____ to buy a new car right now?

2 I'd like to see you at 2:00 today if it's _____ for you.

3 Your room is a(n) _____ mess, so you'd better clean it up!

4 Paris is known for the _____ yellow limestone of its buildings.

5 The house next door is spooky because it's been _____ for so long.

B Expressions and Phrases

B1. Fill in the blank using an expression in the box.

on a first-come-first-serve basis	at the beginning	in that	far from

1 Tickets are limited and will be given out _____.

2 Human beings differ from animals _____ they are self-aware.

3 Something important always happens _____ of a movie, so don't be late!

4 You're _____ solving the problem. You've just made it more complicated.

B2. Complete each sentence with an expression from the reading passages.
   (Change the form of the verb if necessary.)

give out	turn out	be meant to	plan on

1 This book _____ help you prepare your report.

2 I'm _____ throwing a big party for my 40th birthday.

3 I watched a boy _____ pamphlets to people at the corner.

4 I thought I knew him well, but he _____ to be a bad person.

C Summary

Complete the summary with the appropriate words and expressions.

occupied	icon	intended	connects
views	renowned	tenants	once again

The Empire State Building, after the 9/11, is _____ the tallest building in New York. It opened in 1931, but it did not have a successful start: its location, far from transit, kept many prospective _____ from wanting to occupy it. The building's architecture is distinctive, particularly because it was _____ as a docking station for dirigibles. The building remains the _____ of Manhattan.

The Petronas Twin Towers were designed by the _____ architect César Pelli. They opened in 1998 and for a short time were the world's tallest buildings. One tower is _____ by Malaysia's petroleum company, and the other houses corporate tenants. Visitors can enjoy the _____ from the world's tallest two-story skybridge, which _____ the buildings' 41st and 42nd floors.

CHOOSING RELIGIOUS LEADERS

The Search for the Dalai Lama

Pre-reading Activity

Fill in the blanks using the words *roof*, *administered*, and *plateau*.

Tibet is a _____ region in Asia, north of the Himalayas. Tibet is the highest region on earth and it is referred to as the _____ of the world. Today, Tibet is _____ by the People's Republic of China.

According to the ancient customs of Tibet, a new religious and political leader is born each time the previous leader passes away. The Tibetan leader is always a monk referred to as the Dalai Lama. When the 13th Dalai Lama died in 1933, a group of monks and government officials began the search for the baby they believed to be his reincarnation. In the past, this process usually took two to three years, but it took four years to find the 14th Dalai Lama.

The search party follows ancient signs and designated sources of information. The direction that the deceased Dalai Lama's head was facing was one factor involved in the search. In addition, one member of the search party had a vision of the remote Amdo region. This was considered significant, especially because the vision was very detailed with an image of a small hut next to a lake. After a long search, the lake was identified and the hut was found.

One member of the search party had been the previous Dalai Lama's best friend. He walked into the house, and when the child saw him, there was recognition in his eyes. The man was holding many items, and when he showed the child the various items, <u>he</u> was able to choose the ones that belonged to the 13th Dalai Lama. He was taken away from the parents and brought back to the monastery to be raised by the monks. In the winter of 1940, the monks issued a formal <u>proclamation</u>: the Dalai Lama had been found. Since then, the Dalai Lama has earned widespread admiration, not just as the leader of the Tibetan people but as a spiritual leader to people around the world.

1

5

10

15

20

Reading Tips

usage of "issue"

Verb: to announce something officially; to officially make things available for people to buy or use

The president issued a statement to the press.

Noun:

1. a subject that people discuss or argue about, especially relating to society, politics, etc.

   A big issue in the region is that a huge chemical plant will be built.

2. a magazine that is published at a particular time

   The article appeared in the August issue.

1   **What is the passage mainly about?**

     a. old superstitions in Tibet

     b. political conflicts in Tibet

     c. the death of a Tibetan leader

     d. the selection of the Tibetan leader

     e. the party searching for the Dalai Lama

2   **What does the word "he" refer to?**

     a. the 13th Dalai Lama

     b. the 14th Dalai Lama

     c. one of the child's parents

     d. one of the search party members

     e. previous Dalai Lama's best friend

3   **Which is closest in meaning to the word "proclamation"?**

     a. rule

     b. event

     c. legality

     d. entertainment

     e. announcement

4   **Which best fits for the blanks?**

> From the deceased Dalai Lama, the search party found a _____ to find his _____. When the search party found the 14th Dalai Lama, they _____ him to the monastery.

     a. sign, partner, elected   b. clue, successor, took

     c. glimpse, idol, brought   d. hint, predecessor, took

     e. permit, successor, walked

5   **After the 14th Dalai Lama was found, what happened to him?**

_____

CHOOSING RELIGIOUS LEADERS

The Papal Conclave

Pre-reading Activity

True or False?

1. T – F: The Vatican is actually a country.
2. T – F: Its economy is based on tourism.
3. T – F: The Vatican is the same size as Rome.
4. T – F: Over 100,000 people live in the Vatican.

The pope is the leader of the Catholic Church, and when the time comes 1
to find a new pope, there is a very specific election process. A papal conclave, a
special meeting of all the cardinals below the age of 80, is held in the Vatican.
Dating back more than 1,000 years, it is the oldest leadership selection process.

Before the establishment of the papal conclave, the clergy and the people 5
of Rome used to elect the pope. However, due to severe political interference,
no pope was chosen between 1268 and 1271. The resulting <u>fiasco</u> led the ruling
Council of the Roman Catholic Church to decree that the members of the papal
conclave had to be locked in during the selection process! They literally are not
permitted to leave until a new pope has been elected. That tradition continues to 10
this day, although a cardinal may leave if he is ill.

The conclave involves several days of prayer, debate, and voting. Cardinals
do not campaign to be elected pope, although shortlists are often published
and discussed in the media. There are three phases of voting, which eventually
narrow down the choice of candidates to the one meant to be the next pope. He 15
must be elected by a 2/3 majority, though, and there has always been considerable
disagreement. Once the selection has been made, bells ring throughout Rome and
a white smoke signal is given.

There are very strict rules about privacy during the conclave. No reporters
are allowed inside, and during the election of Pope Benedict XVI, the conclave 20
chambers were even scanned in order to find <u>electronic listening devices</u>. There
have been proposals to change the conclave process. Whether or not it happens, it
must be fascinating to observe.

Reading Tips

Below is used when one thing is at a much lower level than another. It can be a preposition or an adverb.

The lake is almost 950 feet below sea level.

Under is used when one thing is at a lower level than another, or is covered by it. It is nearly always used as a preposition.

Her yellow raincoat is under the table.

Underneath often has a similar meaning to under, and is used especially when something is hidden or covered.

The life-jacket is located underneath your seat.

Beneath can be used in the same ways as under and below, but is a more formal word.

She and I live beneath the same roof.

1 **What is the best alternative title of the passage?**

a. Electing the Pope

b. Selecting a Cardinal

c. A Private Meeting of Cardinals

d. Conflicts Between Religions and Politics

e. The History of the Roman Catholic Church

2 **Which is closest in meaning to the word "fiasco"?**

a. mess

b. session

c. omission

d. conclave

e. selection

3 **Which of the following is true?**

a. Most potential popes campaign like politicians.

b. The pope must be elected by a unanimous vote.

c. A long time ago, the Roman government appointed a new pope.

d. At one time, the clergy and Romans elected the pope by themselves.

e. During the election of the current pope, a reporter eavesdropped using a hidden mike.

4 **Why does the author mention "electronic listening devices"?**

a. to make the story less interesting

b. to suggest spy thrillers and movies

c. to show that the media influences the election process

d. to imply that some of the cardinals in the conclave are spies

e. to show how curious some people are about the papal conclave

5 **What is the "papal conclave"?**

A Words

A1. Fill in the blank according to the definition.

majority	disagreement	severe	admiration	previous

1 _____ : a feeling of favorable respect

2 _____ : extremely bad or serious; very strict

3 _____ : the largest part of a group of people or things

4 _____ : coming before something else in time or sequence

5 _____ : a situation in which people have different opinions about something

A2. Choose the most appropriate word for each blank.

1 Do you have a more _____ map of the area? I can't find exact location.

  a. abstract   b. pictorial   c. simple   d. detailed

2 Is there a doctor on the plane? If there is, please _____ yourself!

  a. admit   b. speak   c. identify   d. tell

3 The French Club will _____ a new president and secretary this year.

  a. replace   b. elect   c. undo   d. divide

4 You need to give us a _____ reason why you are here so late at night.

  a. vague   b. flimsy   c. spurious   d. specific

5 Watching the _____ between the two presidential candidates was interesting.

  a. media   b. journalism   c. debate   d. space

A3. Complete each sentence with one of the words from the box.

remote	hut	reincarnation	search party	process

1 Becoming a U.S. citizen is a long, complicated _____.

2 When the ferry sank, the government sent out a _____ right away.

3 The man sitting next to me on the bus said he is the _____ of Elvis.

4 Miranda had never imagined being able to live in such a _____ village.

5 My uncle owns a little _____ by the lake, and he goes fishing there every weekend.

B Expressions and Phrases

B1. Fill in the blank using an expression from the box.

just as	to this day	due to	according to

1 My phone rang _____ I was stepping into the shower.

2 _____ a severe thunderstorm, this flight has been canceled.

3 _____ a reliable source, the stock market will recover in a few months.

4 _____ we don't know exactly why ships disappear in the Bermuda Triangle.

B2. Complete each sentence with an expression from the reading passages.
    (Change the form of the verb if necessary.)

date back to	pass away	narrow down	be involved in

1 We didn't think that he _____ the car accident.

2 The dinosaur bones _____ a time millions of years ago.

3 My grandmother _____ in her sleep at the age of eighty-two.

4 We _____ the list of vacation spots to two places: Bali and Guam.

C Summary

Complete the summary with the appropriate words and expressions.

dating back	continuing	voting	commences
meeting	reincarnation	religious	permitted

By tradition, the _____ and political leader of Tibet is known as the Dalai Lama. When the current Dalai Lama dies, a search process _____, sometimes taking years until the new Dalai Lama is found. This is always a young child, and according to Tibetan custom, he is believed to be the _____ of the previous one. The current Dalai Lama is the 14th, _____ a line of succession dating back to the 1200s.

The pope, the leader of the Catholic Church, is chosen through an ancient election process called the papal conclave. This is the oldest such procedure in the world, _____ approximately 1,000 years. The conclave is a _____ of cardinals below the age of 80, and participants spend several days debating, _____, and praying. They are not _____ to leave until a decision has been made.

THE EDGE OF FASHION

Jean-Paul Gaultier

Pre-reading Activity

Write down the names of some famous designers.

_____

Which country do you think is known for fashion?

_____

Jean-Paul Gaultier has had one of the most influential careers in the   1
modern fashion world. Gaultier, born in 1952 in the southern suburbs of Paris,
never actually received formal training as a designer. He began making fashion
sketches on his own, and when the legendary designer Pierre Cardin saw some of
them in the early 1970s, he was so impressed that he hired Gaultier right away.   5

Gaultier's first solo collection of clothing made its debut in 1976. However,
the daring and provocative designs Gaultier became known for did not appear
until 1981. He was quickly recognized as the enfant terrible, or bad boy, of
French fashion. Americans mostly were not familiar with him until the early
1990s, when he began designing costumes for Madonna. The bustier that   10
Gaultier designed, featuring what came to be known as the "cone bra," made
news all over the world. People were shocked and intrigued, and Gaultier became
an international celebrity.

Gaultier continued to challenge norms within the fashion industry. His
designs were playful, unconventional, and often shocking. His clothes were often   15
based on street wear found in the rough neighborhoods of Paris, and he became
a regular shopper at the capital's secondhand bazaars and rummage
sales, looking for ideas and inspiration. He also liked to challenge
the industry's expectations where models were concerned. In
his shows, instead of hiring very <u>slender</u> and pretty young women   20
and men, he sometimes used heavy-set women, older men, and
people with extensive tattoos. No designer had challenged
industry standards so boldly before, and people loved it.

Gaultier has gone on to design costumes for major films
and music concerts, and his fashions continue to be among   25
the most celebrated in Paris. He is _____ one of the
world's most important living designers.

Reading Tips

relative pronouns "what" and "that"

Relative pronouns are used to introduce a relative clause and refer to a particular thing or person.

1. that
   I brought the book that you asked for.

2. what = the thing that
   I brought what you asked for.

1   **What is the main idea of the passage?**

    a. how to become a fashion designer

    b. Jean-Paul Gaultier's fashion career

    c. Jean-Paul Gaultier's business in Paris

    d. Pierre Cardin's effect on Jean-Paul Gaultier

    e. Comparison between French fashion and American fashion

2   **Which is closest in meaning to the word "slender"?**

    a. slim

    b. small

    c. plump

    d. slanted

    e. beautiful

3   **What can be inferred from the passage?**

    a. Jean-Paul Gaultier likes heavy-set women.

    b. Gaultier designs very normal, traditional clothing.

    c. Designers usually want the models who are slim and beautiful.

    d. In the past, many fashion designers received little formal training.

    e. Gaultier lived in a rough neighborhood of Paris when he was younger.

4   **Which best fits in the blank?**

    a. indisputably

    b. uncommonly

    c. indescribably

    d. unconsciously

    e. independently

5   **What is the purpose of the passage?**

    a. to give an overview of French fashion

    b. to explain the career of Jean-Paul Gaultier

    c. to discuss the evolution of French design trends

    d. to compare Jean-Paul Gaultier and Pierre Cardin

    e. to compare Gaultier with other important fashion designers

THE EDGE OF FASHION

Coco Chanel

Pre-reading Activity

True or False?

1. T – F: Chanel is a famous Italian designer.
2. T – F: She was the founder of the famous fashion brand, Chanel.
3. T – F: She produced the first perfume to have a designer's name attached to it.

Coco Chanel, who founded the famous design house of Chanel, was born 1
in a village in western France in 1883. One of six children, she was born in a
poor house. When she was 12, her mother died and her father left the family. She
and her four surviving siblings were put into an orphanage. In her teens, Coco
was trained as a seamstress, and some of her female relatives taught her more 5
advanced sewing skills.

At the age of 18, she left the orphanage and began working for a tailor. She
had the good fortune to meet a wealthy man from Paris not long after that. He
bought her fine clothes and jewelry, and this inspired her to begin designing on
her own. She started with women's hats, which quickly became popular, and she 10
used that first success to relocate to Paris, where she expanded her business to
include raincoats and jackets. Her clothes were favored by French stage actresses
and society women, but she faced major setbacks, too: the First and Second
World Wars.

Coco was responsible for establishing many important trends in fashion. 15
Her designs focused on simplicity and comfort, a big change from the tight,
<u>confining</u> clothes women had previously worn. Her goal was to give women a
sense of freedom. Rather than changing her clothes with each new season, she
tended to modify the basic design very little, in order to _____. As a result,
many Chanel designs have continued 20
to look good year after year. Her
famous perfume Chanel No. 5 was
the first to feature a designer's name
as well. Her impact on the fashion
world was so great that she was the 25
only designer chosen among TIME
Magazine's list of the most 100 most
influential people of the 20th century.

Reading Tips

found vs. find

found: to establish a company,
organization, school, or city
founded (past) - founded (past
participle)
The law firm was founded in 2008.

find: to discover, get, or see
something
found (past) - found (past participle)
I found your socks under the bed.

1 **What is the main idea of paragraph 2?**

   a. starting Chanel's career
   b. influential French designers
   c. Chanel's unlucky childhood
   d. Chanel's popularity in Paris
   e. effect of World Wars on Chanel's design

2 **Which is closest in meaning the word "confining"?**

   a. metallic
   b. breezy
   c. compact
   d. expensive
   e. comfortable

3 **Which of the following is NOT true?**

   a. One of Coco Chanel's siblings died.
   b. Coco Chanel's family was very poor.
   c. Hats were the first fashion item designed by Chanel.
   d. Coco Chanel's business wasn't affected by the World Wars.
   e. Coco Chanel had a wealthy lover when she was a young woman.

4 **Which best fits in the blank?**

   a. save money
   b. create a timeless look
   c. impress stage actresses
   d. make people look young
   e. make clothes look luxurious

5 **Why do Chanel clothes look good year after year?**

   a. They are simple in design, with few changes from one year to the next.
   b. The fashion house changes the look of the clothes every year.
   c. Public taste is easy for fashion designers to predict.
   d. They are copied by those of many other designers.
   e. They are getting more expensive year after year.

A Words

A1. Fill in the blank according to the definition.

the suburbs	receive	legendary	slender	sibling

1 _____ : a brother or sister

2 _____ : thin in an attractive way

3 _____ : to get or accept something given to you

4 _____ : very famous and well-known for many years

5 _____ : an area near a large city but away from the center of the city

A2. Choose the most appropriate word for each blank.

1 The population of the U.S.A. dramatically _____ due to the post World War II baby boom.

a. remained   b. dispersed   c. decreased   d. expanded

2 When my uncle's business closed last year, it was a major _____ for him.

a. setback   b. excitement   c. achievement   d. accomplishment

3 I like the _____ of Swedish furniture because it doesn't have many decorations.

a. kitsch   b. boldness   c. simplicity   d. heaviness

4 He is _____ brave, as he's saved hundreds of people's lives as a firefighter.

a. indisputably   b. uncertainly   c. slightly   d. a bit

5 This hand-me-down dress has a(n) _____ design, so I can still wear it.

a. unexpected   b. timeless   c. ignored   d. overlooked

A3. Complete each sentence with one of the words from the box.

impressed	daring	secondhand	extensive	comfort

1 It's a good idea to choose a mattress based on _____, not price.

2 A(n) _____ group of art thieves stole the painting in broad daylight.

3 The doctors could not save him because his injuries were too _____.

4 Most of my books come from _____ bookstores, because they're cheaper.

5 I'd always heard this airline was great, but I was not _____ with their service.

B

Expressions and Phrases

B1. Fill in the blank using an expression in the box.

not long after	right away	all over the world	in order to

1 The economic crisis has affected people _____.

2 _____ I started high school, I met my first boyfriend.

3 They got up early _____ catch the train leaving at 6 a.m.

4 If we leave _____, we will avoid the heavy traffic on the freeway.

B2. Complete each sentence with an expression from the reading passages.
(Change the form of the verb if necessary.)

look for	be known as	be familiar with	be responsible for

1 _____ you _____ any Eastern European languages?

2 A careless camper _____ starting the massive forest fire last night.

3 We spent too much time _____ a parking place at the shopping mall.

4 Nowadays, Shawn Corey Carter _____ more commonly _____ the hip-hop artist Jay-Z.

C

Summary

Complete the summary with the appropriate words and expressions.

provocative	comfortable	connections	orphanage
influence	poverty	apprenticed	formal

In the fashion world, Jean-Paul Gaultier has a great deal of respect and _____. He taught himself to sketch, but had no _____ schooling in fashion. He _____ with the house of Pierre Cardin in the 1970s, and debuted his premiere collection in 1976. Ever since, his _____ and brazen designs have attracted attention worldwide.

Coco Chanel, born in _____ in France, became one of the most influential designers in the world. Though she grew up in a(n) _____, she was trained as a seamstress. An affair with a wealthy man gave her first _____ to the fashion world. She made a break with the past by designing _____, liberating women's clothing, and as a result left an indelible impression on the world of fashion.

ENVIRONMENTAL AWARENESS

Saving the Whales

Pre-reading Activity

Did you know?

Whales generally live for forty to ninety years, depending on their species.
The Blue Whale is the largest living animal, at up to 35 m long and 150 tons.
For centuries, whales have been hunted for meat and as a source of raw materials.

For several years, Paul Watson and his group of staff and volunteers have engaged in a campaign almost every winter to find and stop Japanese ships that hunt whales in the name of research. Watson is the captain of a ship called the *Steve Irwin*. He and his crew are dedicated to saving endangered sea creatures. Many of the larger whale species were badly <u>depleted</u> in numbers before the moratorium on commercial whaling was introduced in 1986. And although some species have shown significant recovery since then, others like the Northern Right Whale remain critically endangered.

In February 2009, the sea captain conservationist noted, "For twelve hours our ship, the *Steve Irwin*, has been on the tail of the *Cetacean Death Star*, the Japanese whale killing factory ship the *Nisshin Maru*. Every hour has brought us closer to this monstrous killing machine, this industrialized floating whale abattoir." The Japanese have continued killing whales over the last 20 years under the loophole of "scientific" whaling. Watson contends that research is not the actual intent. Some say that the whale meat ends up on grocery store shelves.

Confrontations between the *Steve Irwin* and the whaling fleet have resulted in two <u>collisions</u> serious enough to make the headlines. The whaling fleet has been accused of using illegal weapons that generate acoustic waves. These made Watson's crew members feel dizzy and disoriented and may have caused ear and eye damage. The Japanese whalers also used powerful water cannons against the *Steve Irwin* crew. In response, the Japanese have accused the *Steve Irwin* of causing the vessels to collide.

The behavior of people on both sides of the issue has been dangerous and controversial. The question that needs to be asked is whether violence against alleged illegal whaling operations is justified.

1

5

10

15

20

Reading Tips

"need" & "want"

Usually the verbs "need," "want" take infinitives as objects. But when "need," "want" take gerunds as objects, the gerund has passive meaning.

The room needs cleaning.

= The room needs to be cleaned.

1 **What is the passage mainly about?**

a. Steve Irwin: the great environmentalist

b. Japanese cruise ship: the *Nisshin Maru*

c. the environmental harm caused by whaling

d. American versus Japanese environmental issues

e. anti-whaling efforts by the crew of the *Steve Irwin*

2 **Which is closest in meaning to the word "depleted"?**

a. led   b. tripled

c. united   d. reduced

e. expanded

3 **Which of the following is true?**

a. Japanese cuisine does not include whale meat.

b. Since 1986, commercial whaling has been prohibited.

c. The *Steve Irwin* crew has always acted in a non-violent manner.

d. The *Steve Irwin* crew is responsible for great environmental harm.

e. The crew of the *Nisshin Maru* probably did not use illegal weapons.

4 **Which best fits in the blanks?**

> Even after commercial whaling was banned, the Japanese are able to _____ hunting whales by _____ it is done for scientific research.

a. stop, asserting   b. claim, denying

c. resist, asserting   d. continue, denying

e. continue, claiming

5 **Why does the author mention the *Steve Irwin*'s collisions with Japanese whaling ship?**

a. to show that laws need to be changed

b. to imply that whale meat is tasty and delicious

c. to show that both sides are acting outside of the law

d. to suggest that the *Steve Irwin* crew should be arrested

e. to imply that the Japanese are worse than the *Steve Irwin* crew

The Great Pacific Garbage Patch

Pre-reading Activity

Did you know?

It takes over 500,000 trees to make the Sunday newspaper in the USA.
In North America, people throw away 2.5 million plastic bottles every hour.
Every year 45,000,000 kilograms of plastic are dumped into the world's oceans.

Imagine taking a ship across the Pacific Ocean. One day you look out at the water and see a layer of garbage that extends all the way to the horizon. This may sound like a nightmare, but unfortunately, it exists. Known as the Great Pacific Garbage Patch, this area of heavily-polluted water covers an area at least twice the size of France and possibly much larger. Where did it come from, though, and what can be done about it?

The North Pacific Gyre is an ocean current that circles clockwise in the northern expanse of the Pacific Ocean. The current passes the West Coast of the United States, the Philippines, and Japan. Garbage from these countries and others is swept out to sea and added to the mass of waste in the center. There is little wind across this central region, so most of the garbage is trapped there by the circulating water.

Approximately 80% of the trash is believed to come from land, with the other 20% dropped from passing ships. The garbage, mostly plastic, comprises bottles, food packaging, discarded packing material, and other waste. Over time, sunlight breaks down the plastic into smaller and smaller pieces. When it is small enough, it is consumed by plankton, fish, marine birds, and other organisms. This plastic builds up in their bodies and sickens or kills them. The pollution affects animals at higher levels of the food chain as well, including humans.

There is hope, however. A plan called *Project Kaisei* has been developed to study the garbage patch and <u>deploy</u> a fleet of ships dragging special nets to clean up the plastic without catching fish. This plan is sponsored by the United Nations, several American universities, and many foundations and private corporations. The waste will be recycled, thus putting a very serious environmental problem to a positive use.

Reading Tips

usage of "current"

noun: a strong movement of river, lake, air in one direction; a flow of electricity through a wire; an idea, feeling, or opinion that a group of people has
The current in the sea was very strong.

adjective: happening or existing now
The current President of the U.S. is Barack Obama.

1 What is the best alternative title of the passage?

a. How to Clean Up the Seas
b. The Oceanic Garbage Gyre
c. The Garbage Problem in France
d. the Pacific Ocean's Best Fishing Spot
e. Garbage Dumped from Passing Ships

2 Which is closest in meaning to the word "deploy"?

a. station
b. deplete
c. explore
d. withhold
e. manufacture

3 What is the author's attitude toward the garbage situation?

a. negative
b. hopeful
c. hopeless
d. despairing
e. pessimistic

4 What is the purpose of the passage?

a. to frighten the reader
b. to make the reader stop eating fish
c. to talk about garbage problems all over the world
d. to make the reader change his or her eating habits
e. to make the reader aware of an oceanic garbage problem

5 Why is the most of garbage trapped in the center of the North Pacific Gyre?

A **Words**

A1. Fill in the blank according to the definition.

engage	significant	commercial	comprise	sponsor

1 _____: having a major effect on someone or something

2 _____: to be made up of a large group of people or things

3 _____: to do or be involved in; to attract someone's attention

4 _____: being connected in business; relating to earning a profit

5 _____: to give money to a group or organization in exchange for advertising

A2. Choose the most appropriate word for each blank.

1 My little sister used to wake up from terrible _____ every night.
 a. desires   b. cravings   c. nightmares   d. appetites

2 The U.S. military _____ a tremendous number of troops after 9/11.
 a. hired   b. corrupted   c. deployed   d. misplaced

3 Many people were _____ by contaminated beef in their hamburgers.
 a. made unaware   b. sponsored   c. nourished   d. sickened

4 We should recycle as much of our trash as possible instead of _____ it.
 a. reselling   b. discarding   c. reusing   d. consuming

5 What can we do to protect _____ animals in the wild?
 a. domestic   b. neutral   c. commercial   d. endangered

A3. Complete each sentence with one of the words from the box.

alleged	justify	current	deplete	moratorium

1 May I have your name and _____ address?
2 Do you think we will _____ our supplies of petroleum soon?
3 It's hard to _____ spending millions of dollars just to throw a party.
4 My boss _____ that our new accountant was stealing from the company.
5 The government declared a(n) _____ on importing medicine from China.

B Expressions and Phrases

B1. Fill in the blank using an expression from the box.

in the name of	in response to	all the way	over time

1 Many terrible things are done _____ business every day.

2 I drove _____ to New Orleans without stopping, so I'm really tired now.

3 I'm writing _____ your request for additional information on our business.

4 _____, the global sea level is rising because of glacier melt and ocean thermal expansion.

B2. Complete each sentence with an expression from the reading passages. (Change the form of the verb if necessary.)

make the headlines	be dedicated to	result in	engage in

1 Some celebrities are experts at _____ via shocking behavior.

2 When the airline's takeover bid failed, it _____ lower stock prices.

3 Foster _____ protecting the world's wildlife when she was younger.

4 The survey shows that 5% of the population _____ voluntary activities on a regular basis.

C Summary

Complete the summary with the appropriate words and expressions.

block	floating	controversy	trapped in
launched	crew	currents	unlawful

The captain and the _____ of the *Steve Irwin* have been attempting to _____ Japanese whaling activities for many years. Their actions have resulted in a considerable amount of _____. There have been a number of confrontations, involving collisions between the ships and the possible use of _____ weaponry.

A large region in the North Pacific Ocean is home to a gigantic mass of _____ garbage. Because ocean _____ pass close to the coasts of several nations and move in a large spiral, litter in the water is _____ the center of the gyre. Most of this trash breaks down in sunlight and is subsequently eaten by marine creatures. A project has been _____ to clean up all the floating garbage.

Language learning is
a part of your journey to academic success.

Fear is the main source of superstition,
and one of the main sources of cruelty.
To conquer fear is the beginning of wisdom.

Bertrand Russell

원서 술술 읽는
Smart Reading

정답 및 **해설**

넥서스영어교육연구소 지음

- ✓ 고급 장문 독해 훈련
- ✓ 흥미 있고 유익한 32개 주제
- ✓ 내신, 수능, TOEFL 대비
- ✓ WORD BOOK 제공
- ✓ 무료 MP3 다운로드
- 💻 www.nexusEDU.kr

1

NEXUS Edu

원서 술술 읽는
Smart Reading

정답 및 **해설**

넥서스영어교육연구소 지음

1

UNIT 1-1 　Economic Rise of China

○ 정답

1. d　2. b　3. a　4. d　5. consumer safety and environmental pollution

○ 해석

중국의 경제는 1970년대 말 이후로 급속히 성장해 왔다. 그전에 중국은 엄격한 공산주의 형태의 정부였다. 하지만, 중국은 인구의 약 53%가 빈곤한 상태에 놓여 있었고, 세계의 다른 국가와 교역이 거의 없었다. 1979년에 시장이 개혁된 이후로 생활수준이 향상되고 있다. 경제 규모는 해마다 더욱더 커지고 복잡해지고 있다. 경제 규모는 사용하는 측정 기준에 따라 세계에서 두 번째이거나 세 번째로 크다. 중국은 놀라운 성취를 이뤄냈지만, 여전히 많은 과제를 가지고 있다.

중국에서는 소비자 안전이 커다란 문제이다. 너무나 많은 사업체가 생기면서 경쟁이 치열해졌고, 모든 사업주는 경쟁에서 앞서 나가기를 원하고 있다. 정부의 안전 규정은 거의 없고 시행하기도 어렵다. 이런 이유로 일부 사업체는 유제품에 멜라민을 첨가하고, 어린이용 의약품에 해로운 화학물질을 첨가하는 등 위험한 방식으로 비용을 절감하고 있다. 결과적으로 다른 나라의 많은 사람은 원산지가 중국인 식품과 약품에 대해 우려하고 있다.

환경 오염 또한 잘 알려진 문제이다. 이는 정부의 느슨한 규제가 낳은 또 다른 결과이다. 중국에서 사용되는 전기의 대부분은 석탄을 원료로 하고, 석탄은 상당한 양의 매연을 만들어 낸다. 석탄을 연료로 사용하는 발전소에서 나오는 연기, 이제는 자동차를 구매할 경제적 여유가 있는 중국인들이 구입한 수백만 대의 자동차에서 배출되는 배기가스와 공장 배출물 때문에 베이징, 광저우, 서안 같은 도시에 드리운 공기는 갈색일 때가 잦다. 중국 정부는 심각한 문제에 직면해 있다는 사실을 알고 이를 해결하려 하고 있다. 예를 들면, 식품과 의약품을 규제하는 새로운 안전 기구가 그것이다. 정부는 새로운 전기원을 조사하고 있다. 주요 도시는 자동차 사용을 줄이려고 지하철을 건설하고 있다. 이런 문제들이 해결될 수 있다면 중국은 오랫동안 번영을 누리는 나라로 존속될 것이다.

○ 해설

1 이 글의 주제는 무엇인가?
　a. 중국의 엄격한 외교 정책
　b. 20세기 이후의 중국의 역사
　c. 중국 정치 체제의 큰 변화
　d. 경제 발전이 중국에 끼친 영향
　e. 중국의 환경오염 문제

2 "prosperous"의 뜻에 가장 가까운 단어는 무엇인가?
　a. 부도덕한
　b. 번영하는
　c. 해로운
　d. 유망한
　e. 거대한

3 이 글에서 유추할 수 있는 내용은 무엇인가?
　a. 중국에서 들여온 의약품은 안전하지 않을 수도 있다.
　b. 중국산 달걀에는 해로운 박테리아가 가득하다.
　c. 냉동 채소 꾸러미 속에서 종종 벌레가 발견된다.
　d. 중국산 의자는 잘 부러져서 의자에 앉는 사람들을 죽인다.
　e. (중국의) 전통 음식인 고기 만두에서 판자가 발견될 수도 있다.

4 중국에서 소비자 안전 문제가 발생하는 이유는 무엇인가?
　a. 많은 노동자가 부주의하다.
　b. 중국에서 품질은 중요하지 않다.
　c. 안전 장비가 너무 비싸다.
　d. 안전 규제가 시행되고 있지 않다.
　e. 인구가 증가하는 것을 막는다.

5 자국의 경제 성장으로 인해 발생한 중국의 문제점은 무엇인가?

○ 구문해설

1행_ China's economy has grown quickly since the late 1970s.

⇨ has grown은 현재완료의 계속적 용법을 나타내며, since는 전치사로 '~ 이래, ~부터' 등의 의미를 갖는다.

11행_ some businesses have cut costs in dangerous ways by adding melamine to dairy products, harmful chemicals to children's medicine,

⇨ by 이하는 전치사의 목적어이다. melamine과 harmful chemicals가 adding의 목적어로 쓰이고 있다.

13행_ As a result, many people in other countries are concerned about food and medicine sourced from China.

⇨ be concerned about은 '걱정하다, 염려하다'라는 의미이다. food and medicine과 sourced 사이에 「관계대명사+be동사」가 생략되었다고 생각하면 문장 구조를 쉽게 이해할 수 있다.

17행_ Because of smoke from coal-burning power plants, exhaust from the millions of cars Chinese people can now afford, and factory emissions, the air over cities like Beijing, Guangzhou, and Xian is often brown.

⇨ smoke from coal-burning power plants, exhaust from the millions of cars Chinese people can now afford, factory emissions는 전치사

of에 연결되어 병렬구조를 이루고 있다. cars와 Chinese people 사이에 목적격 관계대명사 that(which)이 생략되었다.

24행_ Major cities are building subway systems <u>to cut down</u> <u>on</u> automobile use.

⇨ to부정사의 부사적 용법 중 목적을 나타내어 '자동차 사용을 줄이기 위해'라고 해석한다.

UNIT 1-2 A Win-Win Situation

○ 정답

1. a   2. b   3. e   4. d   5. A social entrepreneur seeks to make the world a better place, while also earning a profit.

○ 해석

사업가에 대한 흔한 고정관념은 무슨 수를 쓰더라도 오직 돈을 벌려고 기를 쓰는 매정한 자본가라는 것이다. 하지만, 사회적 기업가라는 새로운 사업 리더로서의 역할이 있다. 사회적 기업가는 이익을 창출하면서도 세상을 더 나은 곳으로 만들려고 노력한다.

전 세계적으로 네 명 중 한 명은 전기 없이 생활하고 있다. 그들은 해가 지고 나면 등유 램프를 사용해야 한다. 하지만, 등유는 비싸고 오염을 일으키며 위험한 가스를 만들어 낸다. 한 사회적 기업가는 세상에 있는 등유 램프를 태양열 LED 램프와 손전등으로 대체하고 싶어 한다. 이런 전등은 낮 동안에 충전해서 밤에 사용할 수 있는 전지가 있는 것이 특징이다. 이들은 대안으로 사용되는 등유 램프보다 비용 면에서 효과적이고 훨씬 깨끗하며 건강에도 좋다. 그의 회사는 그 제품을 판매해서 이익을 남기고 고객은 제품을 사용함으로써 돈을 절약한다. 이는 양쪽 모두에게 이득이 된다.

아마도 세상에서 가장 유명한 사회적 기업가는 무하마드 유누스일 것이다. 2006년 노벨 평화상 수상자인 유누스는 방글라데시 소재 그라민 은행의 설립자이자 소액 금융 분야의 선구자이다. 소액 금융은 가난한 개인이 적은 액수의 돈을 빌려서 새로운 사업을 시작하거나 기존의 사업을 확장할 수 있도록 해주는 과정이다. 유누스는 가난한 자국민에게 자립하는 방법을 보여줌으로써 그들을 돕고 싶어 했다. 그는 그들에게 적절한 조건으로 융자를 제공하고 건전한 재정 원칙을 가르치면서, 이것을 실행해 나갔다. 가난한 사람들이 기존의 일반적인 은행에서 융자를 받는 어렵다. 소액 금융은 상환 위험성이 높아서 처음에는 나쁜 생각인 것 같았다. 하지만 지금은 자리가 잡혔기 때문에 저소득층 사람들이 새로운 사업 기회를 얻을 수 있다.

모든 기업이 이익을 창출하기 위해 존재하기는 하지만, 일부 기업가들은 이익을 창출하는 것과 좋은 일을 하는 것이 상호 배타적일 필요가 없다는 사실을 입증해 보이고 있다.

○ 해설

1 이 글의 제목과 바꿔 쓸 수 있는 가장 적절한 것은 무엇인가?
- a. 좋은 일을 하며 이익을 창출하기
- b. 친환경적인 사업
- c. 훌륭한 방글라데시인 기업가들
- d. 사회적 기업가인 무하마드 유누스
- e. 가난한 나라를 위한 개발 계획

2 항상 사실인 것은 아니지만, (사람들이) 사업가에 대해 흔히 믿고 있는 것은 무엇인가?
- a. 기업가에게 돈은 중요하지 않다.
- b. 기업가는 오로지 돈에만 관심이 있다.
- c. 대부분의 기업가는 학교 성적이 좋지 않다.
- d. 기업가는 교육에 많은 돈을 쓴다.
- e. 기업가는 다른 사람들을 매우 걱정한다.

3 "them"이 가리키는 것은 무엇인가?
- a. 대출금
- b. 적절한 조건
- c. 재정 원칙
- d. 일부 기업가들
- e. 가난한 방글라데시 사람들

4 글쓴이가 상호 배타적이라는 말을 언급한 이유는 무엇인가?
- a. 소액 금융이 위험 부담이 큰 사업임을 암시하려고
- b. 소액 금융이 성공하지 못할 것임을 암시하려고
- c. 사람을 도와주는 일로 돈을 버는 것은 잘못된 일이라고 말하려고
- d. 돈을 벌며 사람들을 도와주는 것이 가능하다는 것을 보여 주려고
- e. 많은 사람이 소액 금융을 통해 도움을 얻고자 한다는 것을 암시하려고

5 사회적 기업가가 하는 일은 무엇인가?

○ 구문해설

1행_ A common stereotype of businesspeople is <u>that</u> they are heartless capitalists <u>who</u> are only out to make a buck,

⇨ that은 접속사로, 명사절을 이끌며 주격보어의 역할을 한다. who는 주격 관계대명사로 선행사는 heartless capitalists이다.

3행_ He or she is seeking to make the world a better place, <u>while</u> also earning a profit.

⇨ 접속사 while은 '~와 동시에'라는 의미로 부사절을 이끈다. 주절의 주어와 부사절의 주어가 같을 경우, 부사절에서 주어와 be동사는 생략할 수 있다.

6행_ However, kerosene <u>is</u> expensive, <u>causes</u> pollution, and <u>creates</u> dangerous fumes.

⇨ is, causes, creates는 모두 본동사로 병렬구조를 취하고 있다.

15행_ Microfinance is the process by which poor individuals are able to borrow small sums of money to start new businesses or expand existing ones.

⇨ Microfinance is the process. Poor individuals ~ existing ones by the process.가 합쳐진 문장으로, 관계대명사 which의 선행사는 the process이다.

21행_ Now that the trend has caught on,

⇨ now that은 접속사로 '~이기 때문에, ~이므로'의 뜻이다.

25행_ While all businesses exist to make a profit, some entrepreneurs have proven that the ideas of profit and doing good don't have to be mutually exclusive.

⇨ 문장의미상 접속사 while은 반대 · 비교 · 대조를 나타내어 '그런데, 한편으로는' 등의 의미로 해석하면 된다. that은 접속사로 명사절을 이끌어 have proven의 목적어 역할을 한다.

UNIT 2-1　Mohandas Gandhi

● Pre-reading Activity

movement, non-violent, influential

● 정답

1. d　2. b　3. b　4. b　5. It was illegal to make their own salt. / All salt had to be bought from the British government.

● 해석

간디는 오늘날 근대 인도의 아버지로 전 세계적으로 잘 알려졌다. 그는 비폭력 시민 불복종 운동을 펴서 대영제국으로부터 인도의 독립을 쟁취하기 위해 성공적으로 싸웠다. 그는 종종 위대한 영혼을 뜻하는 마하트마라는 이름으로 불린다.

1869년에 인도에서 태어난 간디는 열아홉 살이 되었을 때 대학에서 법학을 공부하기 위해 런던에 갔다. 그는 1893년에 남아프리카를 여행했다. 남아프리카 여행은 그의 삶에 전환점이 되었다. 남아프리카에 거주하는 인도인은 많은 외국인 혐오적인 법률의 희생자였고 이런 사실이 간디를 분노하게 했다. 그는 그런 법률에 대항해서 싸우기 위해 비폭력 시위대를 조직했고, 인도인들에게 신분증을 불태우고 정부에 협조하지 말라고 촉구했다. 간디는 이런 유형의 시민 불복종 운동을 벌인 죄목으로 한 번 이상 투옥되었다.

간디는 1915년에 인도로 돌아왔다. 그는 돌아온 즉시 억압적이고 부당한 영국의 지배에 반대하기 위해 시위를 조직하기 시작했다. 영국이 인도인을 끔찍하게 대량 학살한 사건이 벌어졌고 그 이후로 간디는 인도의 독립을 요구하기 시작했다. 간디는 인도인들에게 영국 제품을 사지 말거나 정부 밑에서 일하지 말고, 모든 영국 법률을 무시하라고 말했다. 그가 주도한 시위는 언제나 비폭력적이었지만, 그는 1922년에 투옥되었다.

1930년에 간디와 78명의 추종자들은 직접 소금을 만들고자 바다까지 400킬로미터를 행진했다. 법률에 따르면 모든 소금은 영국 정부로부터 구매해야 했기 때문에 이런 행동은 불법이었다. 이런 시위에 대응해서 영국 정부는 6만 명의 인도인을 투옥했다. 하지만 이 시기에 영국은 인도를 통치하기가 매우 어렵다는 사실을 깨닫고 있었다. 간디가 이끄는 시민들은 세금을 납부하는 것이나 일 하는 것, 정부를 돕는 것과 관련된 일은 무엇이든 거부했다. 1947년에 영국은 인도가 통치 불능 상태에 놓였다는 사실을 깨닫고 간디가 이끄는 인도 정부에 나라의 통치권을 내주었다. 안타깝게도 위대한 영혼은 일 년 뒤에 암살되었다.

● 해설

1 이 글의 주제는 무엇인가?
  a. 모한다스 간디의 남아프리카 여행
  b. 영국 지배하의 인도인의 투쟁
  c. 모한다스 간디가 암살된 이유
  d. 모한다스 간디의 삶과 업적
  e. 모한다스 간디가 인도로 돌아온 이유

2 "outraged"의 뜻에 가장 가까운 단어는 무엇인가?
  a. 기쁘게 했다
  b. 화나게 했다
  c. 우울하게 했다
  d. 이해했다
  e. 기운 나게 했다

3 다음 중 사실은 무엇인가?
  a. 모한다스 간디는 런던에서 태어나 자랐다.
  b. 모한다스 간디는 인도인들에게 신분증을 훼손하라고 부추겼다.
  c. 모한다스 간디는 조국을 위해 영국 정부를 염탐했다.
  d. 간디는 불복종 운동으로 인해 조국에서 추방되었다.
  e. 간디가 암살된 후, 인도는 영국으로부터 독립했다.

4 간디가 인도의 독립을 결심하게 된 직접적인 사건은 무엇인가?
  a. 인도에서 시민전쟁이 일어났다.
  b. 많은 인도인이 영국에 의해서 살해되었다.
  c. 다른 이웃 나라들이 독립했다.
  d. 남아프리카에서 인도 사람들이 많은 외국인 혐오적인 법률로 고통을 받았다.
  e. 영국 정부가 불복종을 이유로 간디를 투옥했다.

5 인도인이 직접 소금을 만들 수 없는 이유는 무엇인가?

구문해설

2행_ He successfully fought for India's independence from Great Britain <u>using a campaign of non-violent civil disobedience</u>.

⇨ using a campaign of non-violent civil disobedience는 분사구문으로 동시 동작을 나타내며, 의미상의 주어는 He이다.

8행_ He organized non-violent protests <u>to fight against</u> the laws, <u>encouraging</u> Indians to burn their identity cards and not to cooperate with authorities.

⇨ to fight against는 to부정사의 부사적 용법 중 목적을 뜻하여, '~에 대항하기 위해'라고 해석한다. encouraging 이하는 분사구문으로 「encourage+목적어+to부정사」의 문장 구조를 취하고 있다.

21행_ the British were finding <u>it</u> very difficult <u>to govern</u> <u>가목적어</u>   <u>진목적어</u>

India.

22행_ <u>The citizens</u>, <u>led</u> by Gandhi, <u>refused</u> to <u>pay</u> taxes, <u>work</u>, or <u>do</u> anything related to helping the government.

⇨ The citizens과 led by 사이에 「관계대명사(who)+be동사」가 생략되었다고 생각하면 문장 구조를 쉽게 이해할 수 있다. 본동사는 refused이며, 동사 pay, work, do가 to에 연결되어 병렬관계를 이루고 있다.

24행_ In 1947, <u>the British</u> <u>found</u> India to be ungovernable and <u>relinquished</u> control of the country to an Indian government <u>headed</u> by Gandhi.

⇨ 주어는 the British, 본동사는 found와 relinquished이다. government와 headed 사이에 「관계대명사+be동사」가 생략되었다고 볼 수 있다.

UNIT 2-2　Abraham Lincoln

Pre-reading Activity

1. Abraham Lincoln, John F. Kennedy, James A. Garfield, William Mckinley

2. four years

정답

1. e　2. e　3. c　4. c　5. a

해석

아브라함 링컨은 어려운 시기에 미국을 능숙하게 이끌었기 때문에 가장 유명한 미국 대통령 중 한 사람이 되었다. 실제로 많은 사람은 당시를 이 신생 국가의 역사에서 가장 어두운 시기 중 하나였다고 생각한다. 링컨은 연합(북부 주들)을 미국 남북전쟁에서 승리로 이끌었고, 노예를 해방시킨 것으로 유명하다.

1809년에 평범한 부모 밑에서 태어난 링컨은 켄터키에 있는 한 농장에서 자랐다. 그는 대통령이 되기 전에 몇 가지 직업에 종사했다. 그는 블랙 호크 전쟁에 대위로 참전했고, 변호업을 했으며, 8년 동안 일리노이 주 국회에서 일했다. 그는 어떻게든 시간을 내서 메리 토드와 결혼했고 네 명의 자녀를 두었다.

링컨은 1858년에 일리노이 주 상원의원 자리를 놓고 스티븐 A. 더글러스와 경선을 벌였지만 패배했다! 하지만, 그는 더글러스와 토론으로 이후 1860년에 대통령 선거에서 승리하는 데 도움이 된 광범위하고 전국적인 지지자를 얻었다. 그는 대통령으로서 자신이 속한 정당을 강력한 국가 조직으로 만들었고, 연방(남부 주들)과 그들의 노예 기반 경제에 반대하려고 다른 단체와 연합을 결성했다.

1861년부터 1865년까지 미국 남북 전쟁은 나라를 분열시키는 위협이 되었지만, 링컨의 확고한 리더십으로 승리를 거두었다. 남북전쟁 중인 1863년 1월 1일에 링컨은 남부 주에서 노예를 영구적으로 해방하는 유명한 '노예 해방 선언문'을 발표했다. 그는 이후 1864년에 대통령에 재선되었다.

링컨은 전쟁과 평화 시기 모두에 위대한 대통령이었다. 링컨은 평화를 정착시키기 위한 계획을 수행하는 데 융통성을 발휘하며 관대했으며, 남부 사람들에게 무기를 내려놓고 다시 합중국에 합세하라고 장려했다. 그의 정책은 분열된 나라를 치유하는 데 도움이 되었다. 링컨은 전쟁이 끝나고 나서 오래 살지 못했다. 링컨은 1865년 4월 14일에 워싱턴 D.C.에 있는 포드 극장에서 존 윌크스 부스에게 암살되었다.

해설

1 이 글의 주제는 무엇인가?

　a. 아브라함 링컨의 정치 파트너들

　b. 아브라함 링컨의 암살

　c. 아브라함 링컨의 재임

　d. 아브라함 링컨의 어린 시절

　e. 아브라함 링컨의 삶

2 "delivered"의 뜻에 가장 가까운 단어는 무엇인가?

　a. 썼다

　b. 가져왔다

　c. 제한했다

　d. 옮겼다

　e. 공표했다

3 이 글에서 유추할 수 있는 내용은 무엇인가?

　a. 링컨은 재선되지 않았다.

　b. 링컨은 훌륭한 군 지도자였다.

c. 링컨은 뛰어난 토론 능력을 지녔다.

d. 링컨은 일리노이 주에 영원히 머물기를 원했다.

e. 링컨의 부모는 워싱턴의 정치인들과 밀접한 관계가 있었다.

4 이 글의 어조는 어떠한가?

a. 무미건조한

b. 편견을 가진

c. 사실적인

d. 향수를 불러일으키는

e. 변덕스러운

5 빈칸에 들어갈 가장 적절한 단어는 무엇인가?

　　　(A)

a. 실제로

b. 그러므로

c. 하지만

d. 더욱이

e. 예를 들면

○ **구문해설**

3행_ Lincoln is known for leading the Union (the northern states) to victory during his country's civil war and for setting the slaves free.

⇨ be known for는 '~으로 유명하다.' lead A to B는 'A를 B로 이끌다'라는 뜻이다. for setting the slaves free는 앞의 is known for와 연결되어 있다.

12행_ in debating with Douglas he gained a wide, national following that later helped him to win the presidency in 1860

⇨ that은 주격 관계대명사로 선행사는 a wide national following이다. help의 목적보어로 to부정사(to win)가 왔다.

19행_ he delivered the famous Emancipation Proclamation that forever freed the slaves within the southern states

⇨ that은 주격 관계대명사로 선행사는 the famous Emancipation Pro-clamation이다.

22행_ Abraham Lincoln was flexible and generous, encouraging Southerners to lay down their weapons and once again join the United States

⇨ encouraging 이하는 분사구문으로 의미상의 주어는 Abraham Lincoln이다. 「encourage A to부정사」는 'A를 ~하도록 장려하다'라는 뜻이며, 동사 join은 앞의 to부정사와 연결되어 있다.

○ **정답**

1. b　2. d　3. c　4. a　5. e

○ **해석**

오랫동안 습관적으로 음식물 쓰레기는 다른 쓰레기와 함께 그냥 버려져 왔다. 음식물 쓰레기는 결국 지역 쓰레기 처리장으로 간다. 그러나 아마추어이지만 매우 혁신적인 일부 정원사들이 음식물 쓰레기를 처리하는 새로운 방법을 발견했다. 지렁이 퇴비가 그것이다. 지렁이 퇴비의 작용 방식은 이렇다. 여러 마리의 지렁이가 들어 있는 용기에 갈기갈기 찢은 젖은 신문을 넣어라. 그리고 나서 음식 찌꺼기를 쓰레기통에 버리지 말고 이 용기에 넣어라. 지렁이가 음식 찌꺼기를 먹고 기본적으로 분해해서 음식물 쓰레기는 눈으로 식별하지 못할 정도가 된다.

하지만, 이것은 시작에 불과하다. 지렁이는 기어가면서 음식 찌꺼기를 먹고 당연히 자신의 쓰레기를 배출한다. 지렁이의 배설물은 매우 유용하다. 그것은 영양이 풍부한 비료가 되므로 정원이나 잔디, 화분에 심은 식물에 사용될 수 있다. 일단 충분한 양의 지렁이 배설물이 생성되면, 사용을 위해 수거될 수 있다. 그리고 나서 새로 신문 조각이 용기에 깔리고 이러한 과정이 다시 시작된다.

지렁이 퇴비가 쓰레기를 줄이는 훌륭한 방법이기는 하지만, 모든 음식물 쓰레기가 지렁이에게 적당한 것은 아니라는 사실을 명심하는 것이 중요하다. 예를 들어, 고기, 기름, 유제품은 복잡하고 쉽게 분해되지 않기 때문에 피해야 한다. 감귤 껍질, 양파, 브로콜리에는 퇴비 과정을 방해하는 천연 화학성분과 효소가 들어 있다. (지렁이 퇴비를 만들기에) 적당한 쓰레기에는 커피 찌꺼기와 종이 필터, 티백, 접시에 남은 음식 찌꺼기, 썩은 과일, 채소 껍질, 남은 음식, 곰팡이가 핀 빵이 포함된다. 지렁이 퇴비가 징그럽게 들릴지 모르지만 이것은 재활용의 자연스러운 형태이다. 더욱이 이것은 쓰레기를 줄일 수 있는 탁월한 방법이다. 무엇보다도 지렁이 퇴비는 멀리 떨어진 장소에서 오래된 채소를 사오지 않고 지역 내에서 좀 더 건강에 좋은 채소를 재배하는 데 도움이 된다.

○ **해설**

1 이 글의 주제는 무엇인가?

a. 음식물 쓰레기를 처리하는 방법

b. 지렁이가 어떻게 음식물 찌꺼기를 재활용하는 것을 도울 수 있는가

c. 지렁이가 먹는 것과 먹지 않는 것

d. 쓰레기를 줄이기 위해 재활용품 사용하기

e. 우리는 어떻게 좀 더 건강에 좋은 과일과 채소를 재배할 수 있는가

2 밑줄 친 "they"가 가리키는 것은 무엇인가?

a. 찌꺼기

b. 정원사

c. 지역 주민

d. 지렁이

e. 과일과 채소

3 다음 중 사실은 무엇인가?

a. 지렁이는 모든 음식물 쓰레기를 먹는다.

b. 지렁이는 오래된 신문지 뭉치를 먹는다.

c. 지렁이는 음식물 쓰레기를 먹고 분해한다.

d. 지렁이는 음식물 찌꺼기를 먹고 열에너지를 발생시킨다.

e. 지렁이가 너무 많은 음식을 먹고 죽으면 비료로 유용하다.

4 "disrupt"의 뜻에 가장 가까운 단어는 무엇인가?

a. 방해하다

b. 조직화하다

c. 위치가 뒤바뀌게 하다

d. 파열시키다

e. 도움이 되다

5 글쓴이가 지역에서 채소를 재배하는 것에 대해 언급한 이유는 무엇인가?

a. 그것은 그 지역의 대기 오염을 증가시킨다.

b. 그것은 더 많은 유기농 쓰레기를 생산한다.

c. 그것은 힘든 일이기 때문에 좋은 운동이 될 것이다.

d. 그것은 아름다운 잔디와 꽃을 재배하는 데 도움을 준다.

e. 운송이 짧아지면 과일과 채소는 더 신선해진다.

◯ 구문해설

1행_ Traditionally, food waste <u>has</u> simply <u>been tossed out</u> with the trash.

⇨ 현재완료의 계속적 용법을 나타내고 있다.

6행_ The worms eat the scraps, essentially <u>causing</u> the food waste <u>to be broken</u> down <u>so that</u> it is unrecognizable.

⇨ causing 이하는 분사구문으로 「cause+목적어+to부정사」의 문장 구조를 취하고 있다. so that은 '그래서, 그러므로'라는 의미로 결과의 부사절을 이끌고 있다.

14행_ it is important to keep in mind <u>that</u> not all food waste
가주어   진주어

     is appropriate for the worms

⇨ 접속사 that은 명사절을 이끌며 목적어 역할을 한다.

15행_ For example, meats, oils, and dairy products should be avoided, <u>as</u> they are complex and don't break down easily.

⇨ as는 접속사로 이유를 나타내어 '~이므로, ~ 때문에' 등의 의미로 쓰였다.

☆ 다양한 as의 용법

Young <u>as</u> he is, he is very smart. (양보)
(그는 어리지만, 매우 똑똑하다.)

Do in Rome, <u>as</u> the Romans do. (양태, 상태)
(로마에서는 로마인처럼 행동하라.)

She came up, <u>as</u> I was watching TV. (때)
(내가 TV를 보고 있을 때 그녀가 왔다.)

UNIT 3-2   Fill'er Up and Order of Fries, Please!

◯ Pre-reading Activity

1. petroleum, propane, ethanol, methanol, biodiesel, electricity, etc.

2. olive, palm, nut, coconut, etc.

◯ 정답

1. b   2. b   3. e   4. d   5. pure vegetable oil and waste vegetable oil

---

◯ 해석

과학자들은 세상에 돌아다니는 차량에 동력을 제공할 수 있는 실현 가능한 대체 연료를 만들기 위해 열심히 노력하고 있다. 에탄올, 수소, 심지어는 압축공기를 포함해서 많은 의견이 제시되고 있다. 하지만 한 아이디어가 많은 사람을 놀라게 할지도 모른다. 바로 식물성 기름이다. 전 세계의 슈퍼마켓과 부엌에서 낯설지 않게 볼 수 있는 흔한 식물성 기름을 곧 주유소에서 찾아볼 수 있을지도 모른다.

자동차를 달리게 하려고 식물성 기름을 사용한다는 개념은 최근 들어서 많이 보도되고 있지만, 이 이론은 1900년대 초에 처음으로 실험이 되었다. 당시에는 1900년도 세계 박람회에서 사람들의 이목을 끌기 위한 선전용 묘기로 행해졌다. 그때는 석유를 식물성 기름으로 대체할 필요가 없었다. 하지만 석유 사용의 부정적 효과가 매우 분명해져서 식물성 기름이 현실적인 대체 연료처럼 보이기 시작했다.

모든 엔진이 식물성 기름을 연료로 해서 달릴 수 있는 것은 아니다. 하지만 식물성 기름은 많은 디젤 엔진에 사용하기 적합하다. 디젤 엔진이 식물성 기름을 연소시키기 위해서는 종종 약간의 개조 과정만을 거치면 된다. 대부분의 경우, 엔진은 기름을 연소시키기 전에 약간 가열시키기만 하면 된다.

현재 일반적으로 사용하는 식물성 기름에는 두 가지 유형이 있다. 첫 번째는 순수한 식물성 기름으로, 식물이나 병에서 바로 나오는 단순한 기름이다. 두 번째이자 훨씬 흥미로운 유형은 식물성 폐유로, 산업용 튀김 프라이팬에서 사용된 기름의 부산물이다. 지역 맥도날드가 감자튀김을 요리하고 나서 남은 기름으로 당신의 자동차를 주행할 수 있다는 것을 생각해 봐라. 하지만 여기에는 의도하지 않았던 부작용이 있을 수 있다. 가까운 미래에는 밖으로 나갈 때마다 더러운 자동차 배기가스를 흡입해서 기침하는 대신에 그저 배가 고플지도 모른다.

◎ 해설

1 이 글의 주제는 무엇인가?
   a. 주유소에서 식사하기
   b. 식물성 기름을 연료로 사용하기
   c. 패스트푸드 음식점에서 주유하기
   d. 새로운 자동차 엔진 기술의 발표
   e. 대체 연료의 개발 과정

2 "put forth"의 뜻에 가장 가까운 단어는 무엇인가?
   a. 제외하다
   b. 제안하다
   c. 생각하다
   d. 제거하다
   e. 잊다

3 다음 중 사실은 무엇인가?
   a. 하이브리드 자동차는 식물성 기름으로 달린다.
   b. 자동차 엔진에 식물성 기름을 사용하는 데 문제가 없다.
   c. 1900년대 초반에 연료로 식물성 기름을 사용하는 것이 유행했다.
   d. 대체 연료로 식물성 기름을 사용하는 것은 어떤 부작용도 없을 것이다.
   e. 순수한 식물성 기름뿐만 아니라 식물성 폐유도 연료로 사용할 수 있다.

4 다음 문장이 들어가기에 가장 적절한 곳은 어디인가?

> 이것은 그렇게 하지 않으면 버려졌을 기름의 참신한 용도이다.

5 우리가 일반적으로 사용하는 식물성 기름의 두 가지 형태는 무엇인가?

◎ 구문해설

8행_ replacing typical gasoline with vegetable oil was unnecessary
⇨ 주어는 동명사구로 단수 취급을 하므로 동사 was가 와야 한다.

9행_ now that the negative effects of using traditional oils have become very apparent,
⇨ now that은 접속사로 '~이기 때문에, ~이므로' 등의 뜻을 가지고 있다.

12행_ Not all engines can run on vegetable oil.
⇨ Not all은 부분부정으로 '모두가 ~은 아니다'라는 의미이다. all, every, both, always 등이 not과 같이 쓰여 부분부정을 나타낸다.
   We do not know everything. (부분부정: 우리가 모든 것을 아는 것은 아니다.)
   We know nothing. (전체부정: 우리는 아무것도 모른다.)
   Not all men are wise. (부분부정: 모든 사람이 현명한 것은 아니다.)
   No men are wise. (전체부정: 아무도 현명하지 않다.)

20행_ It is a novel use of oil that would have otherwise gone to waste.
⇨ that은 주격 관계대명사로 선행사는 oil이다. 부사 otherwise는 '만약 그렇지 않으면'이라는 뜻이다.

21행_ In the near future, instead of coughing from inhaling dirty car exhaust every time you step outside,
⇨ every time 대신에 whenever를 쓸 수 있다.

UNIT 4-1   Four days in the Desert

◎ Pre-reading Activity

the Sahara, Northern Africa

◎ 정답

1. e   2. d   3. e   4. e   5. They stayed with their vehicle and lit a fire to attract attention.

◎ 해석

스코틀랜드 글래스고에서 온 맥도날드 가족이 오스트레일리아 서부에서 휴가를 보낼 때, 래버턴 시에서 북쪽으로 90마일 떨어진 험난한 사막 지대에서 자동차가 고장이 났다. 이 사건이 일어난 것은 화요일이었고 맥도날드 가족은 수요일 저녁에 캘굴리 시에 도착하기로 되어 있었다. 그들이 나타나지 않자, 맥도날드 부인의 남동생이 지역 경찰에게 알렸다.

맥도날드 가족의 자동차를 발견했던 구조 팀의 대변인은, 가족이 사막 여행에 대비해 준비가 잘 되어 있었다고 말했다. 그들은 도움을 청하러 길을 떠나지 않고 자동차 옆에 머물러 있어야 한다는 점을 알았고, 주의를 끌기 위해 불을 피우는 등 올바르게 행동했다. 분별 있는 대응책에는 추운 밤에 대비해서 따뜻한 옷을 가져오고, 해가 뜨거운 낮에 대비해서 가벼운 옷과 모자, 자외선 차단제를 가져가는 것이 포함될 것이다. 더욱이 여행객들은 구급상자, 지도, 성냥이나 라이터, 칼을 포함한 잘 갖춰진 생존 장비를 갖고 있어야 한다. 또한, 충분한 양의 식량과 물, 보조 타이어, 연료 등을 확실하게 준비해야 한다. 대변인의 마지막 권고는 자신의 여행 계획을 친구나 가족에게 알리라는 것이었다.

그 시련을 겪고 나서 존 맥도날드는 오스트레일리아에 오기 전에 사막에서 생존하는 법에 대해 광범위하게 독서를 했었다고 기자들에게 말했다. 그는 가족이 가장 가까운 마을까지 걸어가려 시도했었다면 충분한 양의 물을 소지할 수 없으리라는 사실을 알았다. 맥도날드 부인은 소화에는 많은 양의 물이 소요되기 때문에 가족들이 물을 마시고 음식 섭취를 줄이게 했다. 맥도날드 씨는 구조 팀을 보고 매우 안도했으며 가족이 생존한 것에 감사한다고 말했다. 앞으로 사막으로 여행 갈 다른 사람들에게 어떤 조언을 해줄 수 있는지 질문을 받은 맥도날드 씨는 "허둥대지 마세요. 마음을 진정하고 구조되기를 기다리세요." 라고 말했다. 오스트레일리아 오지를 통과하는 이번 여행은 맥도날드 가족이 결코 잊지 못할 휴가이다!

○ 해석

1 이 글의 주제는 무엇인가?
  a. 오스트레일리아 서부를 방문하는 것에 대한 여행 정보를 제공
  b. 혹독한 (기후) 조건에서 살아남는 방법에 대한 교육
  c. 사막 여행을 준비하는 방법에 대한 자세한 설명을 제공
  d. 사막에서 사람들이 죽을 수도 있는 다양한 상황을 설명
  e. 맥도날드 가족이 사막에서 어떻게 살아남았는지를 설명

2 "rugged"의 뜻에 가장 가까운 단어는 무엇인가?
  a. 건조한
  b. 바위가 많은
  c. 모래투성이의
  d. 험한
  e. 부드러운

3 이 글에서 유추할 수 있는 내용은 무엇인가?
  a. 우리가 사막을 횡단하기 위해서는 특수 차량이 필요하다.
  b. 사막을 횡단하려는 사람들은 숙달된 여행 가이드가 필요하다.
  c. 사막에서 길을 잃으면, 도움을 얻을 수 있는 장소를 찾아라.
  d. 오스트레일리아에서 많은 사람이 여름에 사막을 횡단하다가 길을 잃는다.
  e. 사막에서는 낮과 밤의 기온 차이가 급격하다.

4 빈칸에 들어갈 가장 적절한 단어는 무엇인가?
  a. 그래서
  b. 하지만
  c. 그러므로
  d. 대조적으로
  e. 더욱이

5 맥도날드 가족이 사막에서 자동차가 고장 났을 때 한 것은 무엇인가?

○ 구문해설

6행_A spokesperson from the rescue team that discovered the McDonalds' vehicle said that the family was well-prepared for their desert trek.

⇨ 첫 번째 that은 주격 관계대명사로 선행사는 the rescue team이며, 형용사절을 이끌고 있다.

⇨ 이 문장의 주어는 A spokesperson이며, 본동사는 said이다. 두 번째 that은 접속사로 명사절을 이끌며, 동사 said의 목적어 역할을 하고 있다.

13행_The spokesperson's final recommendation was to tell a friend or family member about your travel plans.

⇨ 주격보어로 to부정사가 왔다.

19행_Mrs. McDonald made sure that the family drank water and reduced what they ate,

⇨ that은 접속사로 명사절을 이끌고 있으며, what은 the thing which로 바꿔 쓸 수 있다.

24행_This trek through the Australian outback is one vacation the McDonald family will never forget!

⇨ one vacation과 the McDonald family 사이에 목적격 관계대명사 that이 생략되었다고 생각하면 문장 구조를 쉽게 이해할 수 있다.

UNIT 4-2   Nerves of Steel

○ 정답

1. e   2. d   3. a   4. c   5. e

○ 해석

담력이 있다는 것은 무슨 뜻일까? 자신의 생명과 많은 타인의 생명이 위험에 처했을 때 어떻게 자제심을 발휘할 수 있을까? U.S. 항공의 기장인 체슬리 B. '설리' 설렌버거는 자신이 조종하는 민간 항공기를 허드슨 강에 부드럽게 착륙시킬 때 이런 침착한 태도를 보이면서 영웅으로 떠올랐다.

설렌버거가 조종하는 에어버스 A-320은 2009년 1월 15일에 뉴욕의 라과디아 공항을 이륙한 지 몇 분 되지 않아서 매우 위험한 상황에 처했다. 기장은 고장 난 항공기를 착륙시킬 수 있는 활주로를 찾기 위해 신속하게 항공 교통 관제탑에 연락을 취했다. 그의 메시지가 공중파 너머로 울려 퍼졌다. "새떼와 부딪쳐서 양쪽 엔진이 추진력을 잃었다. 우리는 라과디아로 회항하겠다." 관제관들은 U.S. 항공 1549편이 착륙할 활주로를 찾기 위해 발 빠르게 움직였다. 기장은 번개처럼 신속하게 결정을 내리고 "우리는 허드슨 강에 착륙하게 될지도 모릅니다."라고 발표했다. 당황한 비행기 탑승객들은 "충격에 대비하십시오."라고 말하는 기장의 차분한 목소리를 들었다. 비행기의 승객들은 자신의 생명을 낯선 사람의 수중에 맡겼을 때 최고로 긴장했다. 후에 기장은, 인구가 조밀한 지역에 추락하는 참사의 위험을 감수하지 않고 강에 불시착했다고 연방 항공국에 보고했다. 다행히 페리가 근처에 있어서 탑승객 155명 전원이 구조되었다. 승객들은 노련한 에어버스 조종사에게 칭찬을 아끼지 않았다. 정작 설렌버거는 인터뷰 기자에게 자신은 해야 할 일을 했을 뿐이

라고 말했다.

설렌버거는 허드슨 강에 착륙한 날에 미국의 영웅이 되었다. 그는 버락 오바마 대통령의 영접과 축하 인사를 받았다. 셀렌버거를 축하하는 행사가 2009년 1월 24일에 그의 고향인 캘리포니아 주 댄빌에서 열렸고, 그 행사에서 그는 영웅적인 행동으로 상을 받았으며 명예 경찰관으로 임명되었다. 그가 여러 해에 걸친 경험과 강심장을 소유한 것이 얼마나 감사한 일인지 모른다!

● 해설

1 이 글의 주제는 무엇인가?
a. 항공 안전에 대한 논의
b. U.S. 항공기에 관한 이야기
c. '강심장'이라는 어구에 대한 설명
d. 비행기 추락에서 살아남기 위한 방법을 논의
e. 기장 체슬리 셀린버거에 대한 이야기

2 "crippled"의 뜻에 가장 가까운 단어는 무엇인가?
a. 전부 갖추어진
b. 선출된
c. 팽창한
d. 파손된
e. 위험한

3 체슬리 셀린버거에 대한 글쓴이의 태도는 어떠한가?
a. 찬미하는
b. 부정적인
c. 희망적인
d. 중립적인
e. 사실적인

4 이 글의 목적은 무엇인가?
a. 독자에게 경고하려고
b. U.S. 항공이 가진 문제점에 대해 이야기하려고
c. 체슬리 셀린버거의 영웅적인 착륙에 대해 이야기하려고
d. 독자에게 항공 안전 문제를 인식시키려고
e. 뉴욕 공항으로 비행하려는 독자의 마음을 바꾸려고

5 다음 문장이 들어갈 가장 적절한 곳은 어디인가?

> 하지만, 라과디아 공항으로 돌아가기에는 시간이 충분하지 않았다.

● 구문해설

7행_ The pilot quickly contacted air traffic control to find an available runway on which to land his crippled aircraft.

⇨ to find는 to부정사의 부사적 용법 중 목적을 나타내어 '찾기 위해서'라는 뜻이다.

⇨ 선행사가 시간, 장소, 방법을 나타내는 명사일 때, 「전치사+관계대명사+to부정사」의 형태로 올 수 있다. 이때 전치사와 관계대명사는 생략할 수 있다.

18행_ Passengers had nothing but praise for the skilled airbus driver.

⇨ nothing but은 'only(그저 ~일 뿐)'의 의미이다.

20행_ Sullenberger became an American hero the day he landed in the Hudson River.

⇨ the day와 he 사이에 관계부사 when이 생략되었다.

22행_ in his hometown of Danville, California, where he was presented with an award and named an honorary police officer for his heroics

⇨ 관계부사 where는 in which로 바꾸어 쓸 수 있으며, 상이 수여되었고 명예 경찰로 임명된 것이라는 의미이므로 수동의 문장이 와야 한다. presented와 named는 병렬구조로 수동형으로 쓰였다.

24행_ Thank goodness he had years of practice and nerves of steel!

⇨ goodness와 he 사이에 접속사 that이 생략되었다고 생각하면 문장 구조를 쉽게 이해할 수 있다.

UNIT 5-1   Bringing Back "Aloha"

● 정답

1. e 2. a 3. c 4. b 5. e

● 해석

하와이에는 공식 언어가 영어와 하와이어 두 개이다. 하와이어는 태평양 너머 피지와 필리핀 같은 지역에서 사용되는 언어와 매우 비슷하다. 하와이어는 거의 소멸된 언어에 가까워졌지만 말이다.

하와이어의 쇠퇴에는 많은 요인이 있다. 무엇보다도 1700년대 후반에 탐험가들이 도착하고 1800년대 초반에 선교사들이 도착하면서 새로운 문화와 아이디어뿐만 아니라 질병도 들어왔다. 이런 질병에 면역성을 가지고 있지 않았기 때문에 많은 지역 주민들이 죽었다. 하와이어를 말하는 원주민의 수가 급격하게 감소했다. 둘째, 하와이 군주제가 폐지되었고, 1896년에는 영어가 학교와 정부의 공식 언어가 되었다. 미국인 인구가 계속 늘어나면서 영어가 상용 언어가 되었고 더 나아가서 하와이어의 사용이 제한되었다. 해가 거듭하면서 하와이어의 소리가 거리에서 점점 사라지게 되었다.

하와이가 1959년에 미합중국으로 편입되었을 때, 사람들은 하와이어를 공식 언어에 포함시키기 위해 투쟁했다. 현재 더욱더

많은 수의 하와이 사람들이 조상이 대대로 사용했던 언어를 배우려 애쓰고 있고, 하와이 주 정부가 그들을 돕고 있다. 현재 학교에서 하와이어를 가르치고, 하와이어 신문이 발간되고, 하와이어로 방송하는 라디오 프로그램도 몇 개 있다. 심지어 새 하와이어 사전까지 만들어졌다. 그 중에서도 정부가 하와이어를 보호하기 위해 시도하고 있는 참신한 방법 중 하나는 니하우 섬에 관광객을 들이지 않는 것이다. 니하우 섬에서 하와이어는 니하우 섬 주민들이 유일하게 사용하는 언어이다!

비록 하와이어가 소멸 위기를 모면하기는 했지만, 이를 사용하는 사람은 인구의 1.5%에 불과하다. 하와이 섬에서는 일어와 필리핀어인 타갈로그가 훨씬 광범위하게 사용되고 있다. 하와이어는 아직도 갈 길이 멀다. 하지만, 당신이 (하와이를) 방문했을 때 사람들이 "헬로!"라고 말하지 않고 하와이어인 "알로하!"라고 말하는 소리를 듣게 될 것이다.

◉ 해설

1 이 글의 주제는 무엇인가?
   a. 하와이의 정치 현황에 대한 조사
   b. 하와이에서 사용되는 언어에 대해 논의
   c. 하와이어의 소멸 역사를 제공
   d. 타갈로그, 일어, 하와이어를 비교 대조
   e. 하와이어의 배경과 현황을 설명

2 "extinct"의 뜻에 가장 가까운 단어는 무엇인가?
   a. 사장된
   b. 현존하는
   c. 번영하는
   d. 감소하는
   e. 줄어드는

3 다음 중 사실이 아닌 것은 무엇인가?
   a. 하와이에서 영어 이외에 다른 언어도 쓰여진다.
   b. 하와이에서는 하와이어가 공식 언어이다.
   c. 1959년 이래로 하와이어를 사용하는 하와이 사람의 수가 감소했다.
   d. 주 정부는 하와이어의 소멸을 막으려고 애쓰고 있다.
   e. 서구에서 들어온 질병이 하와이어를 하는 원주민 감소의 원인되었다.

4 하와이어의 부활에 대해 글쓴이의 태도는 어떠한가?
   a. 무관심한
   b. 낙관적인
   c. 냉담한
   d. 중립적인
   e. 즐거워하는

5 글쓴이가 니하우 섬의 여행 제한을 언급한 이유는 무엇인가?
   a. 니하우가 하와이의 일부가 아니라는 것을 암시하려고
   b. 니하우가 관광객에게 매혹적인 섬이 아니라는 것을 암시하려고
   c. 니하우 섬에서 영어가 너무 많이 사용되고 있다고 말하려고
   d. 니하우의 언어가 하와이어와 다르다는 것을 말하려고

   e. 하와이 정부가 하와이어를 보호하기 위해 강력한 조처를 취하고 있다는 것을 보여 주려고

◉ 구문해설

1행_ The Hawaiian language is very similar to languages spoken across the Pacific Ocean in places like Fiji and the Philippines.
⇨ languages와 spoken 사이에 「관계대명사＋be동사」가 생략되었으며, like는 전치사로 '～ 같은, ～처럼' 등의 뜻을 가지고 있다.

11행_ English became the language of business, further limiting the use of Hawaiian
⇨ 분사구문으로 의미상 주어는 앞 문장 전체를 의미한다.

14행_ the people fought to have Hawaiian included as an official language
⇨ 「사역동사(have)＋목적어＋p.p.」의 구문으로, 하와이어가 포함된다는 뜻이다. 목적어와 목적보어는 수동의 관계이므로 과거분사 included가 왔다.

19행_ One particularly novel way the government is trying to protect the language is by not allowing tourism to the island of Niihau.
⇨ 위 문장의 주어는 one particularly novel way이며, 본동사는 두 번째 is이다. novel way와 the government 사이에 관계부사가 생략되었다고 생각하면 문장 구조를 쉽게 이해할 수 있다.

27행_ you might hear people using the Hawaiian word "aloha" instead of "hello."
⇨ 지각동사(hear)의 목적보어로 현재분사(hearing)가 쓰였다.

UNIT 5-2 Hieroglyphics

◉ Pre-reading Activity

1. F   2. F   3. T

◉ 정답

1. e   2. d   3. b   4. b   5. things people saw every day: plants, animals, buildings, and people

◉ 해석

대부분의 사람들은 이집트의 피라미드나 스핑크스를 찍은 사진을 보았지만, 피라미드 안에 새겨진 작은 그림이 무엇을 뜻하는지 아는 사람이 있을까? 이집트어는 수 세기 동안 수수께끼였다.

마침내 사람들이 이집트 상형문자를 해독하기까지는 많은 연구와 운이 필요했다.

상형문자라는 단어는 '신성한 언어' 또는 '신의 언어'를 뜻한다. 이집트 상형문자는 처음에는 사람들이 매일 보는 사물, 즉 식물, 동물, 건물, 사람을 그린 그림으로 시작했다. 이런 그림들이 후에 말이 되고 글자가 되었다. 이집트어는 세계에서 가장 오래된 언어 중 하나로 약 5천 년 동안 사용되었다. 하지만 이집트어는 10세기에서 11세기 사이에 사라졌고, 아랍어로 대체되었으며 상형문자에 대한 모든 해석은 자취를 감췄다.

이집트 상형문자의 해독은 운 좋게도 로제타돌을 발견함으로써 가능해졌다. 로제타돌은 1799년에 알렉산드리아 시 근처에서 한 프랑스 군인에 의해 발견되었다. 로제타돌에는 서로 다른 세 언어인 이집트 상형문자, 이집트 민간 문자, 그리스어가 적혀 있다. 로제타돌의 중요성은 정확하게 똑같은 내용이 세 가지 다른 언어로 적혀 있다는 점이다. 역사가들은 그리스어로 씌여진 내용을 읽을 수 있었고, 그리고 나서 똑같은 내용을 상형문자로 읽을 수 있게 되었다. 그들은 로제타돌을 가지고 모든 이집트 상형문자를 해석할 수 있게 되었다.

1824년에 장 프랑수아 샹폴리옹은 상형문자에 대한 책을 출판했고, 상형문자를 해독한 공로로 많은 상을 받았다. 많은 사람들이 도움을 주었지만 상형문자를 해독하는 전체 과정은 몇 년이 걸렸다. 오늘날 전 세계 교수들이 샹폴리옹의 책을 이용해서 이집트 문자를 읽고 있다. 당신도 읽을 수 있다! 미라의 무덤 벽에 쓰인 글자를 읽거나 이집트 상형문자로 비밀 메시지를 보내는 방법을 알고 싶다면 온라인을 살펴보라.

◎ 해설

1 이 글의 주제는 무엇인가?
  a. 고대 이집트의 역사 수업
  b. 상형문자와 다른 문자 체제를 비교
  c. 그림이 문자의 한 형태가 되는 방식
  d. 영어와 상형문자 간의 번역 수업
  e. 상형문자의 역사적인 배경 정보

2 로제타돌에 대한 사실은 무엇인가?
  a. 그것은 그리스 학자가 썼다.
  b. 그것에는 상형문자 사전이 들어 있다.
  c. 그것은 이집트의 민간 문자로 된 번역을 제공했다.
  d. 그것은 상형문자와 그리스어로 된 똑같은 내용의 글을 보여 주었다.
  e. 그것은 초기 영어의 형태로 쓰였다.

3 "crack"의 뜻에 가장 가까운 단어는 무엇인가?
  a. 시작하다
  b. 풀다
  c. 부서지다
  d. 녹이다
  e. 질문하다

4 빈칸에 들어갈 가장 적절한 말은 무엇인가?

> 오랫동안 아무도 이집트 상형문자를 해독할 수 없었다. 로제타돌이 발견되고 나서야 비로소 우리는 이집트 상형문자를 이해할 수 있었다.

  a. 발견할, ~까지, 읽고
  b. 해독할, ~이 되어 비로소, 발견되고
  c. 찾아낼, ~이 되어 비로소, 덮어지고
  d. 이해할, ~까지, 건설되고
  e. 읽을, 전에, 입증되고

5 처음에는 어떤 그림이 고대 이집트어로 사용되었나?
_____

◎ 구문해설

2행_ does anyone know what all the little drawings inside the pyramids mean
⇨ 위 문장은 간접의문문으로 「동사(know)+의문사+주어+동사」의 어순으로 쓰임을 기억하자.

8행_ Egyptian hieroglyphs first began as pictures of things people saw every day:
⇨ pictures of things와 people 사이에 목적격 관계대명사가 생략되었다.

15행_ An understanding of Egyptian hieroglyphs was made possible only by the lucky discovery of the Rosetta Stone.
⇨ 위 문장은 수동형 문장으로, 이를 능동형 문장으로 바꾸면 The lucky discovery of the Rosetta Stone made an understanding of Egyptian hieroglyphs possible.이 된다.

17행_ On the Rosetta Stone is writing from three different languages:
⇨ 부사구 On the Rosetta Stone이 문두로 와서 문장이 도치되었다. 이 문장은 다음과 같이 바꿔 쓸 수 있다.
Writing from three different languages is on the Rosetta Stone.

19행_ The importance of the stone was that the exact same message was written in the three different languages.
⇨ that은 접속사로 명사절을 이끌어 주격보어 역할을 하고 있다.

27행_ Check online to see how you can read the walls of a mummy's tomb, or send a secret message in Egyptian hieroglyphics.
⇨ 위 문장은 간접의문문으로 「동사(see)+의문사+주어+동사」의 어순으로 쓰임을 기억하자. 동사 send는 조동사 can과 연결되어 동사원형이 왔다.

UNIT 6-1   Reality Television

○ 정답

1. d   2. e   3. d   4. a   5. b

○ 해석

최근 들어 리얼리티 텔레비전이 매우 인기를 끌고 있다. 인테리어 디자인, 패션, 음악, 요리, 댄스 등 거의 모든 관심 분야에 적합한 리얼리티 텔레비전 프로그램이 있다. 텔레비전 방송망에서 리얼리티 프로그램이 차지하는 대중성과 수익성은 누구도 반박할 수 없다. 다른 한 편으로, 프로그램 구성 가치로서 합법성은 자주 논쟁의 대상이 되고 있다.

리얼리티 텔레비전은, 익살꾼이 낯선 사람들에게 했던 짓궂은 장난을 촬영하기 시작한 1948년경부터 우리와 함께 해왔다. 리얼리티 텔레비전은 이렇듯 시작은 변변치 못했지만 1990년대 초반에 이르러 완전히 다른 모습으로 변화했다. 오늘날의 리얼리티 프로그램은 흥미를 조성하기 위한 방법으로 굴욕과 갈등에 의존한다. 프로그램의 내용이 반드시 대본으로 작성될 필요는 없지만, 제작자들은 긴장을 조성하기 위해 서로 다른 배경과 이념을 가진 사람들을 의도적으로 선택한다. 이런 긴장은 시청자들을 흥분하게 한다. 이는 폭력, 논쟁, 히스테리, 기타 미심쩍은 행동의 형태로 나타난다. 시청자들이 참가자들의 행동을 지켜볼 때, 리얼리티 텔레비전은 시청자들에게 그들이 보는 것이 정상적이고 적절한 행동이라는 메시지를 전달한다. 결국 리얼리티 텔레비전은 무례하고 이기적인 사회를 구축하는 데 일조할지도 모른다.

과거에 사람들은 단순히 농담을 하고 텔레비전을 보면서 재미있게 시간을 보내는 것으로 행복을 느꼈다. 리얼리티 텔레비전은 방영 시간이 길어질수록 더욱 도가 지나치게 된다. 매 시즌이 끝날 때마다 제작자들은 시청률을 높이기 위한 새로운 방법을 찾는다. 오늘날, 시청자들은 한 시즌에 최소한 한 번 이상 물리적인 싸움을 보기를 기대한다. 현재의 상승률로 볼 때 앞으로 높은 시청률을 달성하기 위해 무엇이 필요하게 될지는 단지 상상에 맡길 뿐이다. 우리가 이런 현상을 멈추고 사회를 보호하는 유일한 방법은 리얼리티 텔레비전을 폐지하는 것이다.

○ 해설

1 이 글의 주제는 무엇인가?

a. 10대에게 미치는 텔레비전의 나쁜 영향

b. 더 많은 리얼리티 텔레비전 쇼의 요청

c. 리얼리티 텔레비전의 폭력과 나쁜 행동

d. 리얼리티 텔레비전과 리얼리티 텔레비전이 사회에 미치는 영향

e. 리얼리티 텔레비전과 다른 형태의 텔레비전 프로그램을 비교

2 "suit"의 뜻에 가장 가까운 단어는 무엇인가?

a. 하다

b. 해치다

c. 입다

d. 요구하다

e. 충족시키다

3 이 글에서 유추할 수 있는 내용은 무엇인가?

a. 요즘 사람들 대부분은 텔레비전을 너무 많이 본다.

b. 10대들은 리얼리티 텔레비전 쇼의 참가자들을 따라한다.

c. 사회 과학자는 리얼리티 텔레비전 쇼를 지지한다.

d. 리얼리티 텔레비전의 의도적인 구성이 사회에 영향을 끼친다.

e. 텔레비전은 대중의 행동에 거의 영향을 끼치지 않는다.

4 리얼리티 텔레비전에 대한 글쓴이의 태도는 어떠한가?

a. 비평적인

b. 중립적인

c. 긍정적인

d. 지지하는

e. 동정적인

5 빈칸에 들어갈 가장 적절한 말은 무엇인가?

	(A)	(B)
a.	많아질수록 …	더 좋아진다
b.	길어질수록 …	더 많아진다
c.	길어질수록 …	더 적어진다
d.	많아질수록 …	더 적어진다
e.	적어질수록 …	더 길어진다

○ 구문해설

3행_ The popularity and profitability of reality programs for television networks are something that no one can refute.

⇨ that은 목적격 관계대명사로 선행사는 something이다.

7행_ Reality television has been with us since about 1948, when a prankster started filming practical jokes he played on strangers.

⇨ has been은 현재완료의 계속적 용법으로 1948년 이후 계속해서 리얼리티 텔레비전이 존재했다는 뜻이다. jokes와 he 사이에 목적격 관계대명사가 생략되었다.

14행_ When viewers watch the participants act, it sends a message to viewers that what they are seeing is normal, appropriate behavior.

⇨ 지각동사(watch)의 목적보어로 동사원형(act)이 왔으며, that은 접속사로 명사절을 이끌며, a message의 동격이다. that절의 주어는 what they are seeing이며 단수 취급하여 본동사는 is가 왔다.

19행_ The longer reality television stays on the air, the more outrageous it gets.

⇨ 「the + 비교급 ~, the + 비교급 …」은 '~하면 할수록 더욱 …하다'라는 뜻이다.

UNIT 6-2 Gossip Media

◉ Pre-reading Activity

Paparazzi, celebrity

◉ 정답

1. c   2. e   3. d   4. d   5. They are not sure that the media has the right to publicly announce private information about celebrities.

◉ 해석

신문이나 인터넷, 텔레비전 뉴스를 흘끗 보기만 하더라도 공인에게 그다지 사생활이 없다는 사실을 쉽게 알 수 있다. 매일 흥미진진한 새로운 가십 거리가 나돌고, 가십 거리에는 체면을 손상시키는 사진과 때로는 비디오까지 동반하는 경우가 종종 있다. 매체의 가십난은 자체적인 산업이 되면서 큰 사업으로 자리 잡고 있다.

이토록 광범위한 인기를 끄는 것이라면 이를 비판하는 사람도 항상 있다. 이런 경우에 사람들은 유명인에 대한 사적인 정보를 공공연하게 발표할 권리가 매체에 있는지 의문을 던지고 있다. 하지만 몇몇 사람들은 영화배우와 기타 연예인들이 공인으로서의 삶을 살겠다고 의식적으로 결정을 내렸다고 주장한다. 오늘날의 세계에서는 사생활이 거의 없다. 유명인에 대한 흥미진진한 사진과 이야기는 많은 돈을 벌어들일 가치가 있을 수 있고, 파파라치는 오랫동안 계속해서 사진을 찍어 왔다. 심지어 어떤 사람은 이것이 명성을 얻으려면 치러야 하는 대가라고 말하기도 한다.

이런 상황에 약간의 위선이 개입되기도 한다. 이런 유명인과 사회 인사의 대부분은 경력의 초기에 자신을 드러내기 위해 매체를 적극적으로 활용했다. 이는 경력 초기에 출세하기 위한 전략이었다. 또한, 유명인의 개인 정보가 기사화로 이어지는 경우에 많은 유명인은 의도적으로 신상 정보를 누설하여 명성을 얻고자 했다. 일단 유명해지고 나자 그들의 태도가 변했다. 갑자기 매체는 성가신 존재가 되었고, 이런 유명인들은 사생활을 원했다.

가십 매체는 유명인에 대해 보도함으로써 대중에게 봉사하고 있다. 가십 매체의 인기가 그 증거이다. 사람들은 부자와 유명인의 생활방식에 흥미를 느끼고 여기에 매료된다. 유명인이 가

십 대상이 되는 것에 불편한 감정을 느낀다면 해결책은 간단하다. 집중 조명을 받는 직업을 추구하지 말아야 한다.

◉ 해설

1 이 글의 주제는 무엇인가?
  a. 파파라치는 누구인가
  b. 사생활을 원하는 사람들
  c. 가십 매체와 가십 매체의 존재 이유
  d. 가십 매체 산업과 가십 매체 산업의 전망
  e. 개인 정보를 비밀로 하도록 사람들을 장려

2 "compromising"의 뜻에 가장 가까운 단어는 무엇인가?
  a. 더러운
  b. 신이 나는
  c. 동의하는
  d. 교섭하는
  e. 곤란한

3 빈칸에 들어갈 가장 적절한 말은 무엇인가?

4 잠재적 유명인을 위한 글쓴이의 충고는 무엇인가?
  a. 구입 가능한 가장 빠른 차를 사고, 경호원을 고용하라.
  b. 배우나 가수가 아닌 작가가 되어라. 작가에게는 아무도 관심을 가지지 않는다.
  c. 기자에게 쫓기고 싶지 않다면 로스앤젤레스에 가지 마라.
  d. 파파라치가 싫다면, 연예계에 종사하지 마라.
  e. 마스크, 선글라스, 가발을 항상 착용하라.

5 일부 사람들은 왜 유명인사 가십 잡지와 웹사이트를 비평하는가?

◉ 구문해설

1행_ A glimpse at a newspaper, the Internet, or a TV newscast makes it easy to see that public figures don't
　　　　　　　　　　　　　　　　　　　가목적어
have much privacy.

⇨ that은 접속사로 명사절을 이끌며, 동사 see의 목적어 역할을 하고 있다.

16행_ One could even say that this is the price to pay for fame.

⇨ that은 접속사로 명사절을 이끌며, 동사 say의 목적어 역할을 하고 있다.

20행_ Many also sought fame by intentionally revealing personal information, if it meant getting a story written about them.

⇨ 대명사 it은 revealing personal information을 지칭한다.

22행_ Their attitudes changed once they became famous.

⇨ once는 접속사로 '일단 ~하면'이라는 뜻이다.

⇨ interested와 fascinated는 병렬관계를 이루고 있으며, the rich and famous는 rich and famous people를 의미한다.

UNIT 7-1 Chameleons

● **Pre-reading Activity**

1. T   2. T   3. T   4. F

● **정답**

1. e   2. a   3. d   4. b   5. d

● **해석**

카멜레온은 도마뱀의 일종이며 색깔을 바꾸는 능력으로 가장 잘 알려져 있다. 이 매혹적인 능력과 더불어 카멜레온에게는 먹이를 잡기 위해 사용하는 독특하고 복잡한 혀가 있다. 또한 카멜레온은 독립적으로 움직이는 눈이 있다. 눈이 독립적으로 움직이지 않는 인간과 달리, 카멜레온은 한꺼번에 두 방향을 볼 수 있다! 카멜레온은 아프리카, 유럽의 일부, 아시아, 북아메리카에서 발견된다. 그들은 비록 따뜻한 기후를 필요로 하지만, 사막뿐만 아니라 열대우림에서도 발견된다.

카멜레온이 색깔을 바꾸는 이유는 많다. 자신의 주변 환경과 조화를 이루는 카멜레온의 능력에 많은 사람이 매료당한다. 모든 종은 아니지만 카멜레온의 일부 종은 색깔 변화를 가능하게 만드는 특수 세포층을 갖고 있다. 색깔 변화의 가장 분명한 용도는 위장하기 위한 것이다. 카멜레온은 녹색, 갈색, 검은색, 회색, 크림색, 노란색처럼 자연에서 볼 수 있는 색채 대부분에 적응할 수 있다. 일부 카멜레온은 전혀 어려움 없이 주황색, 분홍색, 붉은색으로 변할 수 있다. 다른 카멜레온은 매우 복잡한 패턴을 발달시키기도 한다. 이런 이유가 포식동물로 하여금 카멜레온을 발견하기 어렵게 만들기는 하지만, 이것이 색깔 변화의 유일한 이유는 아니다.

어떤 카멜레온에게 색깔은 자신의 생리적 상태를 표현하는 용도로 사용된다. 카멜레온은 화가 나 있거나 겁을 먹고 있을 때, 싸움에서 이기고 있을 때, 짝을 찾고 있을 때, 색깔이 변할지도 모른다. 이런 색깔 변화는 통제 가능한 것이 아니라 반사 작용으로 발생한다. 카멜레온은 시력이 매우 좋다. 카멜레온의 눈에 있는 렌즈는 카메라의 망원 렌즈처럼 사물을 확대할 수 있다. 카멜레온은 자외선도 볼 수 있다. 그들은 색깔의 미묘한 변화를 감지할 수 있기 때문에 이렇듯 강력한 신호 체계를 발달시켰다. 일부 과학자들은 이런 능력이 먼저 생겼고, 색깔을 보호용

위장의 한 형태로 사용하는 능력이 나중에 발달했다고 믿는다.

● **해설**

1 이 글의 주제는 무엇인가?
   a. 카멜레온이 색을 바꾸는 방법
   b. 카멜레온의 색이 변하는 이유
   c. 카멜레온을 발견할 수 있는 장소
   d. 카멜레온의 자연 서식지
   e. 카멜레온과 카멜레온의 색을 바꾸는 능력

2 "spot"의 뜻에 가장 가까운 단어는 무엇인가?
   a. 발견하다
   b. 잡다
   c. 사냥하다
   d. 도망치다
   e. 점선으로 나타내다

3 빈칸에 들어갈 가장 적절한 말은 무엇인가?
   　　　(A)　　　　(B)
   a. 채택하다 … 섬세한
   b. 식별하다 … 거대한
   c. 변경하다 … 거대한
   d. 적응하다 … 미묘한
   e. 탐색하다 … 작은

4 이 글에서 유추할 수 있는 내용은 무엇인가?
   a. 카멜레온은 육식성이다.
   b. 카멜레온의 색은 무의식적으로 바뀔 수 있다.
   c. 카멜레온은 건조한 지역에서 서식할 수 없다.
   d. 카멜레온은 자신을 보호하기 위해서만 색깔을 바꾼다.
   e. 카멜레온의 눈의 움직임은 사람의 눈의 움직임과 같다.

5 글쓴이가 카멜레온이 여러 색을 나타낼 수 있음을 언급한 이유는 무엇인가?
   a. 다른 동물이 같은 능력을 지니고 있음을 암시하려고
   b. 카멜레온 한 마리가 이 모든 색을 나타낼 수 있음을 말하려고
   c. 카멜레온이 모두 같은 종이 아님을 암시하려고
   d. 카멜레온이 때때로 다양한 색을 통제할 수 있음을 암시하려고
   e. 카멜레온의 색의 변화가 주변 환경에 의해 제한을 받는다는 것을 알려 주려고

● **구문해설**

2행_ chameleons have distinctive, complex tongues <u>that are</u>
     used to catch prey

⇨ that은 주격 관계대명사로 선행사는 distinctive, complex tongues이다. to catch는 to부정사의 부사적 용법 중 목적을 나타내어 '~하기 위해서'라고 해석한다. 「be+used+명사(동명사)」와 구별해야 한다.

8행_ Chameleons' ability to blend in with their surroundings
     has made many people fascinated with them.

⇨ 위 문장의 주어 ability가 단수이므로 본동사는 has가 왔다. made의 목적보어로 과거분사 fascinated가 온 것에 유의하자. 그들을 매혹시키는 것이 아니라 그들에게 매혹 당하는 것이므로 목적보어는 수동의 형태가 되어야 한다.

12행_ Chameleons can adapt to most of the hues found in nature:

⇨ 과거분사 found가 명사 the hues를 후치 수식하고 있다.

26행_ Some scientists believe that this ability came first, and the ability to use color as a form of protective camouflage came later.

⇨ that은 접속사로 명사절을 이끌어 동사 believe의 목적어 역할을 하고 있다. that 이하의 명사절은 중문으로 접속사 and로 연결되어 있다.

UNIT 7-2　Elephants

◉ Pre-reading Activity

land, live, different, distinguishing

◉ 정답

1. d　2. d　3. d　4. a　5. e

◉ 해석

코끼리의 지성을 과소평가해서는 안 된다. 그들은 뛰어난 기억력과 예술적인 재능으로 축복을 받은 탁월한 동물이다. 코끼리는 하루에 대략 495파운드에 달하는 풀을 소비한다. 그들은 하루에 열여섯 시간을 먹는 데 소비하지만, 먹이를 찾아서 하루에 4마일 정도를 걸어야 한다. 이렇듯 먹이에 대한 극도의 필요는 코끼리에게 큰 부담이 된다. 평균적으로 코끼리는 대략 70년 정도 생존하며 탁월한 기억력 덕택에 30년 전에, 심지어 아기 코끼리였을 때 발견했던 장소도 기억할 수 있다.

코끼리들은 이동하면서 먹이를 찾는 다른 코끼리들을 만나기도 한다. 일부 코끼리는 우호적이만, 그다지 우호적이지 않은 코끼리도 있다. 코끼리는 전에 만났던 코끼리를 전부 기억한다. 아마도 심지어 30년 동안 본 적이 없는 코끼리도 알아볼 수 있을 것이다. 그들은 그 코끼리가 위협적인 존재인지, 아니면 친구가 될 수 있을지를 즉시 기억해 낸다.

먹이를 찾고 있지 않을 때 코끼리는 가끔 코로 모래에 그림을 그린다. 그들은 그저 긴장을 풀고 모래에 그림 그리기를 즐기는 것처럼 보인다. 하루는 코끼리 사육사가 이런 현상을 알아채고 코끼리가 무엇을 하는지 보기 위해 붉은색 페인트를 가득 묻힌 그림붓을 코끼리에게 주었다. 사육사는 바닥에 캔버스를 놓고

코끼리가 그 위에 그림을 그릴 것인지 지켜보았다. 정말로 코끼리가 그림을 그렸고, 그때 이후로 동물원에 서식하는 코끼리 대부분에게 붓과 물감, 캔버스가 주어지고 있다. 그 결과 그려진 추상화는 전 세계에서 높은 가격에 판매되고 있다. 기금은 동물원에 서식하는 코끼리를 먹이기 위한 후원금으로 쓰인다. 사람들 대부분은 코끼리가 추상화만을 그릴 수 있다고 생각했다. 하지만 코끼리들은 나무, 꽃, 그 밖에 다른 자연의 생물을 그리는 훈련을 받고 있다. 이를 통해 우리는 '코끼리의 천재성'을 훨씬 많이 이해할 수 있게 되었다.

◉ 해설

1 이 글의 제목과 바꿔 쓸 수 있는 가장 적절한 것은 무엇인가?
　a. 정글의 아티스트
　b. 코끼리의 무덤
　c. 굉장한 대식가인 코끼리
　d. 지적인 동물인 코끼리
　e. 코끼리의 숨겨진 여행 이야기

2 "underestimated"의 뜻에 가장 가까운 단어는 무엇인가?
　a. 비난해서는
　b. 평가해서는
　c. 과대평가해서는
　d. 과소평가해서는
　e. 과장해서는

3 다음 중 사실이 아닌 것은 무엇인가?
　a. 코끼리는 하루의 대부분을 먹는 데 소비한다.
　b. 코끼리는 음식을 찾기 위해 먼 거리를 걸을 것이다.
　c. 코끼리는 자신이 만난 모든 코끼리를 기억할 것이다.
　d. 코끼리의 수명은 인간의 수명보다 훨씬 더 길다.
　e. 코끼리는 30년 전에 음식을 발견한 장소를 기억할 수 있다.

4 빈칸에 들어갈 가장 적절한 단어는 무엇인가?
　a. ~인지 아닌지
　b. ~을
　c. ~하는 동안
　d. ~을
　e. 비록 ~일지라도

5 빈칸에 들어갈 가장 적절한 말은 무엇인가?

> 코끼리는 매우 영리해서 오래 전에 만났던 코끼리를 알아볼 수 있다. 그들은 또한 코를 사용해서 그림을 그릴 수 있다.

　a. 말할, 귀
　b. 볼, 입
　c. 냄새를 맡을, 코
　d. 그림을 그릴, 눈
　e. 알아볼, 코

구문해설

1행_ They are brilliant <u>creatures</u> <u>blessed</u> with both excellent memory and artistic talent.

⇨ 과거분사 blessed가 명사 creatures를 후치 수식하고 있다. creatures와 blessed 사이에 「관계대명사+be동사」가 생략되었다고 생각하면 문장 구조를 쉽게 이해할 수 있다.

6행_ its sharp memory <u>allows</u> <u>it</u> to remember locations <u>where</u> it has found food <u>as long as</u> thirty years earlier, even as a baby

⇨ 「allow+목적어+to부정사」의 문장 구조를 알아두자. where는 in which로 바꿔 쓸 수 있으며, as long as는 '～만큼 오래'라는 의미이다.

8행_ they come across other <u>elephants</u> also <u>looking</u> for food

⇨ 현재분사 looking이 명사 elephants를 후치 수식하고 있다. elephants와 looking 사이에 「관계대명사+be동사」가 생략되었다고 생각하면 문장 구조를 쉽게 이해할 수 있다.

9행_ Elephants remember every <u>elephant</u> <u>they</u> have ever met.

⇨ every elephant와 they 사이에 목적격 관계대명사가 생략되었다.

16행_ The zoo-keeper put a canvas on the ground to see <u>if</u> the elephant would paint on it.

⇨ 위 문장에서 접속사 if는 '～인지 아닌지'의 뜻이다.

UNIT 8-1 Streetcars

Pre-reading Activity

1. F   2. T   3. T

정답

1. d   2. a   3. c   4. d   5. a

해석

오늘날, 많은 도시에서 가장 흔한 교통수단은 버스이다. 어떻게 그렇게 되었는지 생각해 본 적이 있는가? 1800년대 말부터 1940년대에 이르기까지는 시가 전차가 버스보다 광범위하게 사용되었다. 시가 전차는 도시의 거리에 놓인 선로를 따라 달리는 작은 기차이고, 동력원은 머리 위에 교차하여 설치된 전기선이다. 미국의 모든 대도시에는 전차 노선이 교차하고 있었다. 1936년과 1950년 사이에 내셔널 시티 라인스라는 회사가 모든 시가 전차 회사를 사들이기 시작했다. 내셔널 시티 라인스

는 캘리포니아 스탠더드 오일, 제너럴 모터스, 파이어스톤 타이어처럼 시가 전차를 버스로 대체해서 이익을 얻을 수 있는 많은 기업에 의해 세워졌다. 그렇게 내셔널 시티 라인스는 시가 전차 노선을 폐지할 수 있는 구실을 얻었던 것이다.

이런 현상이 피닉스, 디트로이트, 뉴욕 시, 볼티모어를 포함한 미국의 45개 도시에서 발생했다. 비록 1947년에 제기된 소송으로 음모가 밝혀지기는 했지만, 제거된 시가 전차 노선을 복구하기에는 너무 늦었다. 게다가 내셔널 시티 라인스를 지원하고 있는 기업들은 버스 운행으로 많은 돈을 벌어들이고 있었다. 다행히 도시 지도자들이 이제는 이런 경향을 되돌리고 있다. 샌프란시스코, 보스턴 같은 소수의 도시가 시가 전차 서비스를 유지하면서 현재 새로운 노선을 추가하고 있다. 로스앤젤레스 같은 다른 도시들은 시가 전차를 운행했던 노선에 철로를 복구하고 있다. 시가 전차는 교통수단으로서 많은 장점이 있다. 시가 전차는 전기로 작동되기 때문에 도시의 공기를 오염시키지 않고 부드러우면서 조용한 승차감을 제공한다. 어째서 도시가 구식 교통수단을 다시 복구하려고 하는지 의아하게 생각하는 사람이 있을 수도 있다. 아마도 시가 전차는 처음에 좋은 생각이었고 절대 대체되지 말았어야 했다.

해설

1 이 글의 주제는 무엇인가?

   a. 시가 전차로 되돌리는 것에 대한 옹호

   b. 미국 도시의 대중 교통수단에 대한 논의

   c. 버스가 시가 전차보다 뛰어나다는 것을 제안

   d. 시가 전차의 역사와 이점에 대한 논의

   e. 버스가 대중 교통수단으로 부상하게 된 것을 설명

2 "conspiracy"의 뜻에 가장 가까운 단어는 무엇인가?

   a. 음모

   b. 이유

   c. 변명

   d. 대답

   e. 출석

3 다음 중 사실이 아닌 것은 무엇인가?

   a. 시가 전차는 전기로 움직이는 작은 기차이다.

   b. 시가 전차는 현대 도시에서 아직도 운행되고 있다.

   c. 최초의 시가 전차는 1900년대에 설치되었다.

   d. 1940년 이후로 미국의 도시에서 버스가 일반화되었다.

   e. 1920년대에는 미국의 많은 대도시에 시가 전차 노선이 있었다.

4 내셔널 시티 라인스는 왜 모든 시가 전차 시스템을 샀는가?

   a. 도시를 발전 방식을 바꾸려고

   b. 시가 전차 시스템을 지하철 시스템으로 교체하려고

   c. 사람들에게 대중 교통수단을 이용하도록 장려하려고

   d. 시가 전차 시스템을 폐쇄하고 버스 운영으로 돈을 벌려고

   e. 많은 전차를 한 번에 관리하여 시가 전차 시스템의 효율성을 증가시키려고

5 다음 문장이 들어갈 가장 적절한 곳은 어디인가?

> 그들은 시가 전차의 인기를 감소시키기 위해 시가 전차의 노선을 서서히 줄여나갔고, 사람들이 시가 전차를 타지 않게 되면서 전차 노선은 수익성을 잃게 되었다.

◉ 구문해설

2행_ Have you ever thought about how that happened?

⇨ 현재완료의 경험을 나타내며, 전치사 about의 목적어로 간접의문문이 왔다.

5행_ Streetcars are small trains that run along tracks laid in city streets,

⇨ that은 주격 관계대명사로 선행사는 small trains이다. 과거분사 laid가 명사 tracks를 후치 수식하고 있다.

15행_ as people stopped riding them, they became unprofitable

⇨ 접속사 as는 '~이므로, ~ 때문에'라는 의미로 이유를 나타낸다.

18행_ Moreover, the companies backing National City Lines were making a lot of money from buses.

⇨ 현재분사 backing이 명사 companies를 후치 수식하고 있다.

22행_ Others, like Los Angeles, are restoring tracks to the routes where the streetcars used to run.

⇨ 관계부사 where를 in which로 바꿔 쓸 수 있다.

UNIT 8-2 　The Space Elevator

◉ 정답

1. d　2. e　3. d　4. b　5. inside a space station or in a moon hotel

◉ 해석

세계적인 일류 우주 물리학자의 한 사람인 브라이언 루압스터는 화성 엘리베이터라 불리는 발명품을 개발하고 있다. 이것을 시각화하기 위해서 사람들은 '잭과 콩 나무'라는 이야기를 상상하고 싶을지도 모르겠다. 이는 하늘까지 닿는 콩 나무를 키운 한 소년의 이야기이다. 잭은 콩 나무를 타고 올라가서 또 다른 세계에 들어갔다. 우주 엘리베이터는 이와 비슷하지만, 물론 훨씬 첨단 기술이고 게다가 실재한다!

우주 물리학자들은 대양의 플랫폼에 부착시킬 강철 같은 리본이나 케이블을 고안하고 있다. 이 케이블은 우주로 끌어올려져 서 우주 정거장에 부착되도록 고안된다. 2020년이 되면 사람들은 이 엘리베이터를 타고 오르내리며 여행을 할 수 있을 것이다. 우주 엘리베이터가 많아서 관광객과 기업들이 우주로 여행할 수 있게 될 것이다. 평범한 우주 관광객이 우주에 가려면 가장 가까운 바다의 엘리베이터 입구까지 가면 된다. 우주여행은 일주일 정도 걸릴 것이다. 우주 관광객이 우주에 도착하면 우주 정거장 안에 있을 것이고, 그곳에 체류할 수 있을 것이다. 다른 선택 사항도 있다. 천문학자들은 우주 정거장에서 달까지 쉽게 여행할 수 있어서, 우주 관광객들이 달에 세운 호텔에 머물 수 있으리라 생각한다. 그 호텔은 현재 설계 단계에 있다.

당신과 같은 잠재적 우주 관광객을 위한 장래는 밝아 보인다. 산업체와 과학자의 미래 또한 밝아 보인다. 채광 기업은 지구에는 희박한 광물들을 채굴하기 위해 우주로 여행을 갈 것이다. 에너지 과학자들은 지구를 선회할 우주 태양 전지판을 쏘아 올리기 위해 우주로 여행을 갈 것이다. 태양 전지판은 태양으로부터 엄청난 양의 에너지를 수집해서 지구에 쏘아 보낼 것이고, 우리는 이런 에너지를 난방에 사용하고 우리가 필요로 하는 에너지양을 채울 수 있다.

◉ 해설

1 이 글의 주제는 무엇인가?
- a. 우주여행을 장려
- b. 천문학 수업을 제공
- c. 우주 엘리베이터를 건설하는 방법을 설명
- d. 우주 엘리베이터의 개념을 소개
- e. 정부가 우주 엘리베이터를 건설하도록 지지

2 "orbit"의 뜻에 가장 가까운 단어는 무엇인가?
- a. 빛을 내다
- b. 뒤따르다
- c. 깨닫다
- d. 관찰하다
- e. 선회하다

3 우주 엘리베이터에 대한 글쓴이의 태도는 어떠한가?
- a. 중립적인
- b. 반신반의하는
- c. 회의적인
- d. 낙관적인
- e. 의문을 갖는

4 글쓴이가 '잭과 콩 나무'를 언급한 이유는 무엇인가?
- a. 우주 엘리베이터가 허구임을 암시하려고
- b. 우주 엘리베이터가 어떻게 생겼는지를 연상시키려고
- c. 건축 자재에는 무엇이 포함되는지를 설명하려고
- d. 아이들이 우주 엘리베이터 여행을 즐길 것이라고 말해 주려고
- e. 우주 엘리베이터에 대한 아이디어가 이 이야기에서 왔다는 것을 암시하려고

5 우주 관광객은 우주로 여행을 갔을 때 어디에서 머물 수 있는가?

○ 구문해설

3행_ This is the story of a boy <u>who</u> grew a beanstalk <u>that</u> reached the heavens.

⇨ who는 주격 관계대명사로 선행사는 a boy이다. that 또한 주격 관계대명사로 형용사절을 이끌어 선행사 a beanstalk을 수식하고 있다.

10행_ There will be a <u>number of</u> space elevators <u>so that</u> both tourists and businesses can travel into space.

⇨ a number of는 many의 의미이다. so that은 이유의 부사절을 이끌어 '~해서'의 의미이다.

15행_ Astronomers <u>think</u> <u>it</u> will be easy <u>to travel from the</u>
　　　　　　　　　가주어　　　　　　　　　　진주어

　　　 space station to the moon,

⇨ 동사 think와 it 사이에 접속사 that이 생략되었다.

19행_ Mining companies will travel to space to <u>mine</u> elements <u>that</u> are scarce on earth.

⇨ to mine은 to부정사의 부사적 용법 중 목적을 나타내어 '채굴하기 위해서'라는 의미이다. that은 주격 관계대명사로, 선행사는 elements이다.

UNIT 9-1　Barriers Broken in Tiny Tuva

○ Pre-reading Activity

Margaret Hilda Thatcher

○ 정답

1. d　2. e　3. d　4. a　5. She gathered materials, like rubber and metal, to help the Soviet army.

○ 해석

세상을 좀 더 평등하게 만들기 위해 노력할 때는 사회적인 장애물을 무너뜨리는 것이 중요하다. 오늘날에는 여성 대통령이나 수상을 둔 나라가 많지만, 케르텍 안치마 토카라는 사람에 대해 들어본 적은 없을지도 모른다. 그녀는 왕족이 아닌 여성으로서는 최초로 한 나라의 수장이 되었다. 1912년에 그녀는 지금의 몽골 근처 남부 중앙 러시아에 있는 자치 공화국인 투바에서 극도로 가난한 농가에서 태어났다. 부모님 두 분 모두 문맹이었지만, 케르텍은 읽기와 쓰기를 모두 독학했다. 그녀는 모국어로 몽골어를 사용했고, 곧 러시아어를 유창하게 말할 수 있도록 배웠다. 그녀는 소비에트 정부로부터 장학금을 받고 대학에

진학했고, 투바에서는 극히 소수인 대학 졸업자가 되었다. 그녀는 고향에 돌아왔을 때 그동안 받았던 교육 덕분에 지역 정부에서 막강한 인물이 될 수 있었다. 더욱이 모스크바에 있는 소비에트 연방의 중앙 정부는 그녀를 투바의 지역 정부 내에서 더욱 높은 지위로 계속 승진시켜 그녀의 업적을 포상했다. 28세가 되던 1940년에 그녀는 여성으로서는 최초로 투바 정부의 수장으로 임명되었다. 투바 사람들은 놀라울 정도로 여성 정치인에 대해 편안해했다. 제2차 세계 대전 기간 동안 그녀는 고무와 금속 같은 재료를 모아서 나치 독일에 대항해서 싸울 수 있도록 소비에트 연방을 도왔다. 전쟁이 끝나고 나서 그녀는 시간의 대부분을 사회 발전을 위해 일하고 가난을 퇴치하기 위해 싸우는 데 보냈다.

케르텍은 2008년 11월에 96세의 나이로 사망했다. 그녀는 장수해서, 영국에서 마거릿 대처, 독일에서 안젤라 메르켈 같은 여성이 그들 나라에서 지도자가 되는 것을 보았다. 비록 공산당을 위해 일했다는 이유로 현재 투바에서는 논쟁의 대상이 되고 있지만, 많은 사람들은 환경을 극복하고 성공했던 위대한 여성의 사례로 그녀에게 찬사를 보낸다.

○ 해설

1 이 글의 주제는 무엇인가?
　a. 투바 공화국의 역사에 대한 논의
　b. 케르텍 안치마 토카의 지도 스타일에 대한 논의
　c. 케르텍 안치마 토카와 다른 소련 지도자들을 비교
　d. 케르텍 안치마 토카의 삶과 업적에 대한 논의
　e. 케르텍 안치마 토카와 세계의 다른 여성 지도자들을 비교

2 "autonomous"의 뜻에 가장 가까운 단어는 무엇인가?
　a. 가난한
　b. 사회의
　c. 부유한
　d. 의존적인
　e. 독립적인

3 이 글에서 유추할 수 있는 것은 무엇인가?
　a. 케르텍 안치마 토카는 유능한 지도자가 아니었다.
　b. 케르텍 안치마 토카는 자신의 부모님께 읽기와 쓰기를 가르쳤다.
　c. 케르텍 안치마 토카는 투바에 중요한 개혁을 들여왔다.
　d. 케르텍 안치마 토카는 투바와 러시아 밖에는 잘 알려지지 않았다.
　e. 케르텍 안치마 토카는 여성이었기 때문에 투바의 지도자가 되었다.

4 빈칸에 들어갈 가장 적절한 말은 무엇인가?
　a. 논란이 있는
　b. 성공적인
　c. 가치 없는
　d. 잊혀진
　e. 유명한

5 케르텍 안치마 토카는 제2차 세계 대전 기간 중에 어떻게 소비에트 연합을 도왔는가?

◉ 구문해설

8행_ She went to university on a scholarship from the Soviet government, becoming one of only a few people in Tuva to graduate from college.

⇨ becoming 이하는 분사구문으로 and became으로 바꿔 쓸 수 있다.

14행_ she was appointed as the head of Tuva's government, the first woman to hold that position

⇨ as는 전치사로 역할 · 자격 · 기능 등을 나타내어 '~로서'의 뜻으로 해석한다. to hold는 to부정사의 형용사적 용법으로 명사 woman을 수식하고 있다.

18행_ she spent most of her time working for social progress and fighting against poverty

⇨ 「spend+목적어(시간)+(in) -ing」는 '~을 …에 소비하다'라는 의미이다.

21행_ She lived long enough to see women, like Margaret Thatcher in Great Britain and Angela Merkel in Germany, become leaders of their countries.

⇨ 부사 enough는 형용사, 부사 뒤에서 이들을 수식한다. 지각동사 see의 목적보어로 동사원형 become이 왔다.

☆ He is old enough to go to school.
(그는 학교에 갈 만큼 충분히 나이가 들었다.)

UNIT 9-2 Breaking the Glass Ceiling in India

◉ 정답

1. c   2. c   3. c   4. d   5. d

◉ 해석

'유리천장(glass ceiling)'이라는 용어는 여성과 특정 다른 집단의 구성원들이 자신이 종사하는 직업에서 어떤 지점까지는 승진할 수 있지만, 더 높이는 승진할 수 없다는 개념을 뜻한다. 다행히도 세계에서 가장 위대한 여성 중 한 사람인 인디라 간디는 자신의 성(性)을 바탕으로 하는 현재 상태를 인정하지 않겠다고 결심했다. 아마도 영국으로부터 평화적으로 독립을 쟁취하도록 인도를 도왔던 모한다스 간디에 대해 들어봤을 것이다. 인디라 간디는 모한다스 간디와 아무런 관계도 없지만 두 사람의 정치적 이념은 매우 비슷했다. 그녀 또한 독립을 주창했고 폭력보다는 평화로운 방법에 중점을 두며 행동했다. 인디라 간디는 인도에서 가장 영향력이 있는 집안 출신이고, 그

녀의 아버지는 인도 최초의 수상이었다. 그녀는 겨우 아홉 살일 때 영국의 식민지 통치에 대항해서 싸우는 아버지를 도왔다. 어느 날 간디의 집이 영국 경찰의 감시 대상이 되자 그녀는 중요한 문서를 자신의 학교 가방에 넣어서 집 밖으로 빼내도록 도왔다! 그녀는 좀 더 나이가 들자 장학금을 받고 영국의 옥스퍼드 대학교에 진학했고, 졸업하고 난 후에는 인도 정치에 적극적으로 참여했다. 그녀는 인도 국회 의장이자 정보방송부 장관을 지냈다. 보수적인 인도에서 여성이 이렇게 정치적인 지위에 오르는 것은 유례가 없는 일이었다. 그녀는 1966년에 49세의 나이로 인도의 수상에 선출되었으며, 그 자리에 오른 최초의 여성이자 현재까지 유일한 여성이었다.

간디가 직면했던 주요 문제는 조국을 통일하는 것이었다. 슬프게도 이런 투쟁으로 인디라 간디는 자신의 생명을 내놓아야 했다. 1984년에 인도의 시크교 민족 공동체의 투쟁에 불만을 품은 시크교도인 경호원 두 명이 그녀를 암살했다. 오늘날 그녀는 단지 인도에서뿐만 아니라 전 세계적에서 영웅으로 여겨지고 있다. 한 국제적인 설문 조사에서 그녀는 지난 1천 년의 세월 동안 가장 위대한 여성으로 별 어려움 없이 선정되었다.

◉ 해설

1 이 글의 제목과 바꿔 쓸 수 있는 가장 적절한 것은 무엇인가?
   a. 인도의 가장 훌륭한 지도자
   b. 인디라 간디의 죽음
   c. 인도의 첫 번째 여성 수상
   d. 인도에서 일어난 암살의 역사
   e. 인도에서 정치적 힘을 행사했던 왕조인 간디 가문

2 인디라 간디의 아버지에 대한 것 중 사실인 것은 무엇인가?
   a. 인디라 간디가 죽은 후에 죽었다.
   b. 영국 정부의 스파이였다.
   c. 인디라 간디보다 먼저 수상직을 수행했다.
   d. 영국을 위해 서류를 집 밖으로 몰래 빼냈다.
   e. 인도 정부에서 중요한 직위들을 차지했었다.

3 인디라 간디에 대한 글쓴이의 태도는 어떠한가?
   a. 중립적이다
   b. 냉소적이다
   c. 동경한다
   d. 무관심하다
   e. 비관적이다

4 빈칸에 들어갈 적절한 말은 무엇인가?

> 인디라 간디는 살해되지 않았다면 더 훌륭한 일을 성취했을 것이다.

   a. 실패했을, 암살되지
   b. 성취했을, 권좌에서 밀려나지
   c. 알려졌을, 당선되지
   d. 성취했을, 살해되지

e. 기억되었을, 여성이지

5 국제적인 설문 조사에서 유추할 수 있는 것은 무엇인가?
  a. 설문 조사 대부분은 가치가 없고 부정확하다.
  b. 인디라 간디는 암살당해서 유명해졌다.
  c. 여성 지도자들은 대개 많은 관심을 끌지 못한다.
  d. 인디라 간디의 업적은 상당히 의미 있었다.
  e. 많은 사람이 이미 인디라 간디를 잊었다.

◯ 구문해설

1행_ The term *glass ceiling* refers to the idea that women and members of certain other groups can climb to a certain point in their jobs, but no higher.

⇨ that은 접속사로, the idea를 보충 설명하는 동격의 명사절을 이끌고 있다.

10행_ she did so by focusing on peaceful methods rather than violence

⇨ so는 대동사 did의 목적어로서 '그렇게, 그처럼, 그와 같이' 등의 의미로 쓰였다. A rather than B는 'B라기보다는 A'라는 의미로 "폭력보다는 평화로운 방법으로"라고 해석한다.

19행_ It was unprecedented for a woman to hold such
      가주어
    political positions in conservative India.
      진주어

23행_ Gandhi's main challenge was to bring unity to her country.

⇨ to부정사구가 주격보어로 쓰였다.

23행_ this struggle cost Indira her life:
              간·목   직·목

UNIT 10-1   The Lord of the Rings

◯ Pre-reading Activity

J.R.R. Tolkien

◯ 정답

1. d 2. c 3. b 4. e 5. d

◯ 해석

피터 잭슨이 감독했던 세 편의 영화 때문에 '반지의 제왕'이라는 서사시에 친숙해진 사람이 많다. 2001년과 2003년 사이에 극장에서 개봉된 이 영화는 전 세계 관객들에게 소개되어 사랑

을 받았다. 3부작이 성공하면서 J.R.R. 톨킨이 쓴 원작에 대한 관심이 되살아나고 있다.

원래 톨킨은 '반지의 제왕'을 자신이 그전에 썼던 소설 '호빗'의 속편으로 계획했다. 그 책이 너무나 인기를 끌었기 때문에 그의 출판업자는 그가 이야기를 계속 쓰기를 바랐다. 언어학자과 교수인 톨킨은 자신은 작품을 쓰는 데 시간이 많이 걸린다고 출판업자에 경고했지만, 누구도 '반지의 제왕'을 완성하는 데 12년이 걸리리라고는 예상하지 못했다! 게다가 책은 몇 가지 난관을 극복해야 했기 때문에 출간되기까지는 6년이 더 걸렸다.

톨킨은 이야기를 어떻게 시작할지 결정하는 데 어려움을 겪었다. 비록 몇 가지 시도를 했지만, 톨킨의 마음속에서는 줄거리와 등장인물이 결정되지 않았다. 그는 자신이 원하는 아이디어가 없었고 선택하고 싶은 방향을 결정하는 데 또다시 2년이 걸렸다. 게다가 가르치는 일이 너무 바빴던 나머지 1940년대 초반에 한동안 집필을 중단해야 했다. 그는 1949년에 마침내 집필을 완성했다.

'반지의 제왕'은 한 권의 책으로 집필되었지만, 출간 당시인 1950년대 초의 영국은 아직 2차 세계 대전의 피해로부터 복구되는 중이었다. 종이를 포함해서 많은 중요한 물건들이 부족했다. 종이가 부족했기 때문에 톨킨의 출판업자는 '반지의 제왕'을 세 권의 책으로 분리하기로 결정했다. 그때 이후로 세 권의 책은 약 40개 국어로 번역되었고 전 세계적으로 수백만 권의 책이 판매되었다. 환상적인 아동용 이야기로 시작했던 작품이 지금은 20세기 주요 문학작품으로 여겨지고 있다.

◯ 해설

1 이 글의 주제는 무엇인가?
  a. J.R.R. 톨킨의 생애에 대한 이야기
  b. 독자들에게 (소설) '호빗'을 소개
  c. '반지의 제왕'의 줄거리를 설명
  d. '반지의 제왕'의 출판 배경을 설명
  e. '반지의 제왕'이 세 권의 책으로 출판된 이유를 설명

2 "him"이 가리키는 것은 무엇인가?
  a. J.R.R. 톨킨
  b. 톨킨의 공동 집필자
  c. 톨킨 책의 출판업자
  d. 톨킨의 대학 동료
  e. 피터 잭슨

3 "resolve"의 뜻에 가장 가까운 단어는 무엇인가?
  a. 따르다
  b. 분명하게 하다
  c. 마치다
  d. 떠나다
  e. 쓰다

이 글에서 언급되지 않은 것은 무엇인가?

  a. 톨킨은 대학에서 언어학을 가르쳤다.

  b. 톨킨이 '반지의 제왕'을 쓰는 데 12년이 걸렸다.

  c. 톨킨은 한동안 너무 바빠서 글을 쓸 수 없었다.

  d. '호빗'은 매우 성공적인 작품이었다.

  e. 출판업자가 톨킨에게 '반지의 제왕'을 서둘러 쓰도록 요구했다.

5 글쓴이가 제2차 세계 대전을 언급한 이유는 무엇인가?

  a. 톨킨이 독일인이었기 때문에

  b. 톨킨이 전쟁에 참여했음을 암시하려고

  c. 톨킨이 전쟁에서 죽었음을 암시하려고

  d. 물자의 부족이 얼마나 심각했는지 알려 주려고

  e. '반지의 제왕'의 원본이 전쟁 중에 파괴되었기 때문에

○ 구문해설

2행_ Released to theaters between 2001 and 2003, the films were seen and loved by audiences all over the world.

⇨ 수동 분사구문으로 Being released에서 being이 생략되었으며, 의미상의 주어는 the films이다. 위 문장은 다음과 같이 바꿔 쓸 수 있다.
When the films were released between 2001 and 2003, the film were seen and loved by audiences all over the world.

14행_ He didn't have the ideas he needed, and it took him another two years to decide what direction he wanted to take.

⇨ the ideas와 he, direction과 he 사이에 목적격 관계대명사가 생략되었다.

22행_ Since then, the three volumes have been translated into about 40 languages and have sold millions of copies worldwide.

⇨ since는 전치사로 '~ 이후로'라는 의미이며, have been translated와 have sold는 현재완료의 계속적 용법을 나타내고 있다.

25행_ What began as a fanciful children's story is now seen as a major work of 20th-century literature.

⇨ 선행사를 포함하는 관계대명사 what이 명사절을 이끌어 문장의 주어 역할을 하고 있으며, is가 본동사이다.

UNIT 10-2 Don Quixote

○ Pre-reading Activity

1. Spain   2. knight   3. 1600s   4. Sancho

○ 정답

1. c 2. c 3. d 4. e 5. c

○ 해석

세르반테스의 '돈키호테' 이야기는 아마도 스페인 문학에서 가장 유명한 작품일 것이다. 돈키호테가 쓰였을 당시에 이 작품은 너무나 유명해서 지금의 스페인 지역에서 스페인어가 주요 언어로 확립하는 데 도움을 주었다. 1600년대 초반을 무대로 하는 이 작품은 기사와 기사도에 대한 이야기를 너무나 많이 읽은 후 자신 또한 유명한 기사라고 믿게 된 한 노인의 삶을 따라간다. 그는 근처에 사는 한 가난한 농촌 소녀가 실제로는 둘시네아라는 이름의 아름다운 숙녀라고 스스로 확신한다. 하지만, 그는 그녀에게 이런 사실을 알리지 않는다. 그는 자신의 이웃인 산초 판자와 함께 모험을 찾아 떠나기로 결심하며, 그들의 스페인 여행이 많은 일화로 자세하게 서술되어 있다.

돈키호테의 가장 유명하고 기이한 행동 중 하나는 바로 일반적인 사물을 위험하다고 믿는 성향이다. 예를 들어, 돈키호테의 마음속에서 풍차는 거인이 된다. 독자들은 돈키호테와 산초의 기상천외한 행동을 다룬 이야기를 수 세기 동안 즐겁게 읽고 있다. 독자들은 상황의 실체를 알고 있지만, 돈키호테와 산초는 가공의 세계 속에 산다. 소설을 재미있고 유쾌하면서도 여전히 통찰력 있는 작품으로 만드는 것은 바로 이런 부조화이다.

세르반테스의 이야기는 단지 유머 때문에 유명해진 것이 아니었다. 돈키호테는 우스꽝스러운 인물이기는 하지만, 정직과 용맹의 중요성을 받아들이는 위대한 기사도 정신으로 행동하는 인정 많은 사람으로 묘사된다. 돈키호테는 자신의 친구에게 언제나 인정 많고, 자신이 만나는 모든 사람에게 예의 바르고 정중하며, 사람들이 어떻게 서로를 대해야 하는가를 보여 주는 역할 모델이 되어 왔다. 오늘날에는 돈키호테를 전적으로 우스운 인물로 보지 않고 삶에서 진정으로 중요한 것이 무엇인지 아는 몽상가로 본다.

○ 해설

1 세 번째 문단의 주제는 무엇인가?

  a. 사람들이 서로를 대하는 방법

  b. 기사도의 정의

  c. 소설 '돈키호테'의 진정한 의미

  d. 스페인 문학의 평가

e. 세르반테스가 '돈키호테'를 쓴 이유

2 "insightful"의 뜻에 가장 가까운 단어는 무엇인가?

   a. 실행 가능한

   b. 믿을 수 있는

   c. 통찰력이 있는

   d. 관찰할 수 있는

   e. 무례한

3 둘시네아에 대한 이야기 중 사실인 것은 무엇인가?

   a. 그녀는 대단히 아름답다.

   b. 그녀는 돈키호테와 사랑에 빠졌다.

   c. 그녀는 스페인 출신이 아니다.

   d. 그녀는 돈키호테가 자신을 둘시네아라고 부른다는 사실을 모른다.

   e. 그녀는 돈키호테, 산초 판자와 함께 여행을 다닌다.

4 빈칸에 들어갈 가장 적절한 말은 무엇인가?

   a. 그가 세상을 구해야 한다고

   b. 산초 판자가 자신의 하인이라고

   c. 그가 둘시네아 공주의 보호자라고

   d. 모든 사람들이 자신을 기사로 존경한다고

   e. 일반적인 사물을 위험하다고

5 이 글에서 유추할 수 있는 것은 무엇인가?

   a. 돈키호테는 지리에 능숙했다.

   b. 돈키호테는 예술과 미를 보는 눈이 있었다.

   c. 돈키호테는 불의를 보면 참지 않았다.

   d. 돈키호테는 이웃과 이야기하는 것을 좋아했다.

   e. 돈키호테는 친구들에게 어리석은 사람처럼 보이도록 했다.

구문해설

2행_ it was so popular that it helped establish Spanish as the main language of what is now Spain

⇒ 「so ~ that …」은 '~할 만큼 …하여, 대단히 ~해서 …'라고 해석한다. 동사 help 다음에 동사원형이 올 수도 있다. what is now Spain은 '현재의 스페인'이란 뜻이다.

3행_ Set in the early 1600s, it follows the life of an old man who, after reading too many stories about knights and chivalry, comes to believe he too is a famous knight.

⇒ Set in the early 1600s는 '1600년대 초를 배경으로 했다'는 뜻의 분사구문으로 의미상의 주어는 it이다. who는 주격 관계대명사로 선행사는 an old man이며, believe와 he 사이에 접속사 that이 생략되었다.

15행_ It is this incongruence that makes the novel funny, entertaining, yet still insightful.

⇒ 「It is ~ that」의 강조구문으로, this incongruence를 강조하고 있다. funny, entertaining, insightful이 목적보어로 병렬구조를 이루고 있다.

24행_ Don Quixote is not viewed entirely as a comic character, but a dreamer who knows what is truly important in life

⇒ who는 주격 관계대명사로 선행사는 a dreamer이며, 의문대명사가 이끄는 명사절이 동사 know의 목적어 역할을 하고 있다.

UNIT 11-1 Leaving Cuba

Pre-reading Activity

1. T   2. T   3. T

정답

1. d   2. e   3. b   4. building small, rickety boats and rafts and sailing from the island of Cuba to the state of Florida

5. when they are found at sea

해석

여러 나라로부터 많은 사람들이 다양한 이유로 미국으로 이민을 온다. 미국 정부는 쿠바인을 상당히 존중해서가 아니라 정반대의 이유로 쿠바인의 이민을 장려한다. 미국은 쿠바를 적국으로 생각한다.

미국과 쿠바는 상당히 다른 정치 체제를 가졌다. 피델 카스트로가 쿠바의 지도자가 되었을 때 그의 일부 행동이 미국의 분노를 샀다. 미국 정부는 쿠바 국민의 삶의 질이 모질고, 그들이 정부로부터 받는 억압이 용인할 수 없을 지경이라 생각하기 때문에 미국으로 이민 오고 싶어 하는 쿠바인을 위해 특별 규정을 만들었다. 다른 나라 국민은 길고도 시간이 많이 소요되는 신청 과정을 거치는 반면에, 쿠바에서 온 사람들은 정치 난민으로 간주된다. 그러므로 그들은 통상적이고 매우 지루한 과정을 밟을 필요 없이 미국으로 이민 올 수 있다.

이런 특별한 정책 때문에 많은 쿠바인이 미국으로 몰려들고 있다. 쿠바 정부는 외국의 해안으로 가려고 조국 땅을 저버리는 자국 시민들을 비난하며 그들이 고국을 떠나는 것을 어렵게 하려고 애쓰고 있다. 다수의 쿠바인은 자그맣고 삐걱거리는 보트와 뗏목을 만들어서 쿠바 섬에서 플로리다 주까지 항해를 한다. 이 여행은 매우 위험해서 많은 사람이 바다를 건너려 시도하다가 죽어가고 있다. 1973년에 미국 정부는 이렇게 위험한 방법을 사용해서 바다를 건너오는 쿠바 사람들이 미국에 들어오는 것을 더욱 어렵게 만들었다. 그 해에 미국 정부는 '젖은 발, 마른 발' 정책을 수립했다. 이 정책에 따라서 해상에서 발견된 쿠바 이민자들은 쿠바로 돌아가야 한다. 그들이 육지에서 발견되면 미국에 남을 수 있다.

해설

1 이 글의 주제는 무엇인가?
   a. 미국으로 가는 방법
   b. 쿠바를 탈출하는 데 있어서의 위험 요소들
   c. 다른 나라로의 이민
   d. 쿠바에서 미국으로의 이민
   e. 미국과 쿠바의 정치적 관계

2 "forsaking"의 뜻에 가장 가까운 단어는 무엇인가?
   a. 절약하는
   b. 섬기는
   c. 용서하는
   d. 속이는
   e. 버리는

3 빈칸에 들어갈 가장 적절한 말은 무엇인가?
   a. 때문에
   b. 반면에
   c. 하지만
   d. 그러므로
   e. 게다가

4 "this perilous method"는 무엇을 의미하는가?

5 쿠바 난민들이 쿠바로 돌아가야 하는 때는 언제인가?

구문해설

8행_ the repression they face from their government is unacceptable, the U.S. has set up special rules for those Cubans wishing to immigrate to America

⇨ the repression과 they 사이에 목적격 관계대명사가 생략되었으며, 현재분사 wishing은 명사 Cubans를 후치 수식하고 있다.

10행_ While people from other countries have a lengthy, time-consuming application process, people from Cuba are viewed as political refugees.

⇨ while은 접속사로 주절 앞, 뒤에서 반대·비교·대조를 나타내어 '그런데, 한편으로는' 등의 의미를 가지고 있다. as는 전치사로 역할·자격·기능 등을 나타내어 '…으로서'의 의미를 가지고 있다.

18행_ and many people have died attempting the crossing

⇨ attempting the crossing은 분사구문으로 의미상의 주어는 many people이다.

19행_ In 1973, the United States government made it more
_{가목적어} 가목적어

difficult for Cubans to enter the U.S. by using this
_{진목적어} 진목적어

perilous method of crossing the sea.

UNIT 11-2 The Cuban-American Community of Miami

Pre-reading Activity

1. Spanish   2. bilingual   3. Florida

정답

1. e   2. c   3. b   4. d   5. d

해석

미국에서 쿠바계 미국인의 인구가 가장 많은 곳이 마이애미이다. 쿠바계 미국인이 마이애미에 살기로 결정한 데에는 이유가 있다. 무엇보다도 마이애미는 쿠바에 아주 가까워서 많은 쿠바 이민자들의 이민항이 되고 있다. 게다가 마이애미에는 이미 쿠바계 미국인 사회가 큰 규모로 잘 형성되어 있어서 새로 도착한 사람들은 지역 주민들이 쿠바의 문화와 역사를 이미 알고 있고 이해하는 도시에서 생활하고 일하는 것에 편안함을 느낀다.

마이애미의 한 지역은 너무나 많은 쿠바계 미국인들이 거주하고 있어서 '리틀 하바나'로 불린다. 하바나는 쿠바의 수도이며 리틀 하바나는 마이애미에 있는 쿠바계 미국인 사회의 수도로 불릴 수 있다. 많은 음식점이 쿠바 음식을 전문적으로 만들고, 많은 백화점이 쿠바산 제품을 판매한다. 이 지역에 있는 대부분 학교는 2개 국어를 사용하기 때문에 학생들은 영어와 쿠바의 공용어인 스페인어로 말한다. 리틀 하바나는 쿠바 문화의 모든 측면을 기념하는 영화 및 음악 페스티벌이 열리는 것으로도 유명하다.

마이애미에 거주하는 쿠바계 미국인들은 계속해서 쿠바의 문화적 전통을 소중하게 생각하고 기억한다. 예를 들어, 많은 사람들이 쿠바에서 했던 것처럼 마이애미의 공원에서 도미노와 체스 놀이를 한다. 음악 밴드는 하바네라, 구아라차, 단존과 같은 쿠바의 음악 스타일을 연주한다. 쿠바계 미국인들은 종종 조부모, 부모, 미혼 자녀, 기혼 자녀를 포함한 대가족을 이루어 함께 생활한다. 쿠바계 미국인들은 크리스마스의 이브를 특별한 날로 기념하면서, 이를 '노체 부에나'라고 부른다. 이 즐거운 축제 동안에 가족들은 온종일 함께 지낸다. 가족 중에 한 사람은 통돼지를 굽느라 바쁘고, 아이들은 놀이를 하고 어른들은 쿠바에서 지냈던 옛 시절과 미국에서 지낸 좋은 시절을 회상한다. 노체 부에나는 성대한 파티이다. 이와 같은 전통이 쿠바계 미국인들이 자신의 쿠바 유산을 유지하고 후세에 남기는 데 도움을 준다.

해설

1 세 번째 문단의 주제는 무엇인가?
   a. 쿠바의 전통 음악을 연주하는 밴드

b. 쿠바 사람들이 크리스마스를 축하하는 방법

c. 쿠바의 음악이 미국의 음악에 준 영향

d. 쿠바의 가족 구성원들 간의 관계

e. 쿠바계 미국사람들에 의해서 미국에서 유지된 전통

2 "inhabitants"의 뜻에 가장 가까운 단어는 무엇인가?

a. 하인

b. 난민

c. 거주자

d. 이민자

e. 후손

3 이 글에서 유추할 수 있는 것은 무엇인가?

a. 쿠바 사람들은 고향을 가끔 방문한다.

b. 마이애미에 사는 많은 사람들이 스페인어를 할 것이다.

c. 미국과 쿠바는 친밀하고 우호적인 관계이다.

d. 마이애미는 다른 많은 이민자 집단의 고향이기도 할 것이다.

e. 아마 쿠바계 미국인 대부분이 마이애미 시와 관련된 일에 종사할 것이다.

4 이 글의 형식은 무엇인가?

a. 서사시적인

b. 이야기로 된

c. 설득적인

d. 정보를 제공하는

e. 논쟁적인

5 빈칸에 들어갈 가장 적절한 말은 무엇인가?

(A)

a. 반면에

b. 예를 들어

c. 결과로

d. 게다가

e. 그러므로

◉ 구문해설

11행_ Most schools in this area are bilingual, so students speak both English and Spanish, the official language of Cuba.

⤷ so는 등위접속사로 '그래서, 그러므로' 등의 뜻이 있다. Spanish와 the official language of Cuba는 동격의 관계이다.

12행_ Little Havana is also famous for its film and music festivals that celebrate all aspects of Cuban culture.

⤷ that은 주격 관계대명사로, 선행사는 its film and music festivals이다.

25행_ Traditions such as these help the Cuban-Americans maintain and perpetuate their Cuban heritage.

⤷ 준사역동사 help의 목적보어로 동사원형 maintain과 perpetuate가 왔다.

UNIT 12-1 Night Vision

◉ Pre-reading Activity

1. F   2. F   3. T

◉ 정답

1. b   2. b   3. e   4. a   5. a

◉ 해석

어둠 속에서 동물만큼 잘 볼 수 있으면 좋겠다고 생각해 본 적이 있는가? 액션 영화에서 우리는 등장인물이 어둠 속에서 보이지 않는 물건을 보게 해주는 특수 안경을 쓴 장면을 자주 접한다. 모든 사물은 녹색으로 보이지만, 그 모양과 윤곽은 분명하게 볼 수 있다. 실제로 이런 현상은 동물의 야간 시력이 작용하는 방식과 어느 정도 비슷하다.

동물의 사진에서 안광(眼光)을 보았거나, 빛이 동물의 눈을 비췄을 때 직접 안광을 보았을 수도 있다. 개, 고양이, 다른 많은 동물의 망막의 뒤쪽이나 안쪽에는 '반사판(타페툼 루시둠)'이라 불리는 무지갯빛 조직층이 있다. 이 조직의 목적은 눈 속 더 깊이 빛을 반사하는 것이다. 많은 종(種)은 반사판 덕분에 뛰어난 야간 시력을 갖게 되었으며, 이것은 그들의 먹이 사냥을 돕는다. 종마다 안광의 색은 다르다. 개, 고양이, 너구리의 눈에서 반사되는 빛은 노란색을 띠는 경향이 있다. 쥐, 다른 설치류, 새의 눈은 대개 붉게 빛난다. 다른 동물의 눈은 희거나, 노랗거나, 초록이거나, 분홍빛을 반사할 수도 있다. 각각의 경우에 색깔은 세포 안에 있는 화학물질뿐만 아니라 반사판을 구성하는 세포의 유형과 관계가 있다.

안광은 동물의 야간 시력을 향상시키는 기능을 하지만, 인간은 안광의 다른 용도를 발견해 왔다. 예를 들어, 사람들이 어떤 특정한 종류의 동물을 찾고 있다면 안광이 동물을 식별하는 데 도움이 될 수도 있다. 또한, 안광은 인간이 밤에 빛을 반사하는 물질을 발명하도록 영감을 주었다. 이런 물질을 포함한 표식(strip)은 포장도로에서 튀어나온 부분 같은 위험지대를 조심하라고 경고하기 위한 용도로 사용된다. 인간은 밤에 그다지 잘 볼 수 없지만, 여전히 동물이 가진 이런 매혹적인 특성으로부터 혜택을 얻는 방법을 찾아내고 있다.

◉ 해설

1 이 글의 주제는 무엇인가?

a. 사람의 야간 시력

b. 안광과 안광의 혜택

c. 어둠 속에서 동물이 보는 방법

d. 어둠 속에서의 동물의 안광

e. 동물 세계에서의 다른 색의 눈

2 "augmenting"의 뜻에 가장 가까운 단어는 무엇인가?

   a. 빼는

   b. 증가시키는

   c. 줄이는

   d. 논의하는

   e. 논쟁하는

3 빈칸에 들어갈 가장 적절한 말은 무엇인가?

       (A)   (B)

   a. 하지만 … 사실

   b. 예를 들어 … ~할 때

   c. 게다가 … 대신에

   d. 결과로 … 결과적으로

   e. 예를 들어 … ~에도 불구하고

4 다음 중 사실인 것은 무엇인가?

   a. 사람들이 동물들의 야간 시력을 실용적으로 활용하고 있다.

   b. 야간 투시경은 원래 군용으로 발명되었다.

   c. 동물들의 안광의 색이 다른 것은 빛의 색이 다르기 때문이다.

   d. 야간 투시경을 끼면, 모든 사물이 약간 흐려 보인다.

   e. 낮에 야간투시경을 끼면, 눈에 해로울 수 있다.

5 반사판(타페툼 루시둠)은 동물의 야간 시력을 어떻게 도와주는가?

   a. 눈 속 깊이 빛을 반사해 준다.

   b. 모든 사물을 녹색으로 보이게 해준다.

   c. 어둠 속에서 반짝이고 빛을 발생시킨다.

   d. 밤에 동물이 색깔을 구별할 수 있도록 해준다.

   e. 동물에서 멀리 떨어진 바깥쪽으로 빛을 반사해 준다.

구문해설

1행_ Have you ever wished you could see in the dark as well as an animal?

⇨ 현재완료의 경험을 나타내어 '~을 바란 적이 있는가'라는 뜻이다. you could ~ an animal은 명사절로 동사 wished의 목적어 역할을 하고 있다. wished와 you 사이에는 접속사 that이 생략되었다.

2행_ we often see characters wearing special goggles that reveal things not visible in darkness

⇨ 지각동사 see의 목적보어로 분사 wearing이 왔으며, that은 주격 관계대명사로 선행사는 special goggles이다.

12행_ The light reflecting back from the eyes of dogs, cats, and raccoons tends to be yellow.

⇨ 현재분사 reflecting이 명사 light를 후치 수식하고 있다. 이 문장의 주어 the light가 단수이므로 동사(tends)가 3인칭 단수형으로 쓰였다.

19행_ Also, eyeshine inspired humans to invent substances that reflect light at night.

⇨ 「inspire+목적어+to부정사」의 형태로 동사 inspire는 to부정사를 목적보어로 취한다.

☆ to부정사를 목적보어로 취하는 동사: expect, want, force, ask, order, etc.

   They ordered me to leave the room.
   (그들은 내게 방에서 나가라고 명령했다.)

   I want you to see my friend, Jane.
   (네가 내 친구 Jane을 만나 보았으면 해.)

UNIT 12-2   Extrasensory Perception

정답

1. c   2. b   3. d   4. a   5. e

해석

초감각적 지각, 즉 ESP의 개념은 기록된 역사를 통해 볼 때 많은 인간 문화와 함께 존재해 왔다. ESP는 다섯 가지 감각 이외에 존재하는 일련의 능력을 가리킨다. 이것은 정보를 수집하거나, 멀리 떨어진 물체를 보거나, 환경적인 상황을 통제하기 위해 사용될 수 있다. 비록 ESP가 전 세계 대학과 정부에서 수행하는 과학적 조사의 주제가 되어 왔지만, 그 존재를 입증할 만큼 확실한 자료는 거의 없는 것처럼 보인다. 그럼에도 많은 사람들은 이런 능력이 존재한다고 믿는다.

ESP에 대한 최초의 주요 연구 중 하나는 1930년대에 노스캐롤라이나 주에 있는 듀크 대학교에서 실시되었다. ESP를 좀 더 과학적인 방법으로 언급하려고 '초심리학'이란 용어를 만들었던 J.B. 라인은, 최초로 ESP 연구 분야에 과학적 분석의 원칙을 적용한 사람이었다. 그는 스물다섯 장으로 된 간단한 카드 한 벌인 제너 카드를 사용했다. 각 카드는 원, 정사각형, 물결선, 십자가, 별의 다섯 가지 상징 중 하나의 그림이 새겨져 있다. 각각의 상징이 그려진 카드가 다섯 장씩 있다. 그의 실험에서 피실험자인 '리시버'는 카드를 가지고 있는 사람이 어떤 카드를 쥐고 있는지 추측해야 했다. 라인이 수행한 실험의 결과를 보면 일종의 ESP가 사용되었을 가능성이 있음을 보여 주고 있다. '리시버'들이 통계상 가능하다고 한 수치보다 더욱 많이 맞췄기 때문이다. 하지만 다른 연구자들은 라인이 밝혀낸 결과를 정확하게 반복해 내지 못하고 있다.

그때 이후로 수행된 많은 연구가 실제로 비슷한 결과를 산출하고 있다. 즉 연구 결과는 ESP가 텔레비전에서 보는 초인적 능력이 아니라 실재하는 능력일 수 있다는 아주 희박한 가능성만을 보여 준다. 여전히 몇몇 사람들은 이런 자료가 충분한 증거라고 믿는다. 훨씬 더 강력한 증거가 있어야 한다고 믿는 사람도 있다. 이런 논쟁이 해결되든 아니든 우리는 사람들이 언제나 ESP에 매혹되리라는 사실을 확신할 수 있다.

해설

1 두 번째 문단의 주제는 무엇인가?
  a. 특별한 연구 방법들
  b. 제너 카드를 치는 방법
  c. 초감각적 지각에 대한 라인의 실험
  d. 초감각적 지각에 대한 연구가 실패한 이유
  e. 초심리학의 발명가인 J.B. 라인

2 "replicate"의 뜻에 가장 가까운 단어는 무엇인가?
  a. 멈추다
  b. 복제하다
  c. 생산하다
  d. 고려하다
  e. 초기화하다

3 빈칸에 들어갈 가장 적절한 말은 무엇인가?
  a. 유사하게
  b. 그러므로
  c. 게다가
  d. 그럼에도 불구하고
  e. 예를 들어

4 초감각적 지각 연구에 대한 글쓴이의 태도는 어떠한가?
  a. 중립적이다
  b. 의심스럽게 생각한다
  c. 회의적이다
  d. 낙관적이다
  e. 비관적이다

5 글쓴이가 통계치를 언급한 이유는 무엇인가?
  a. 초감각적 지각이 모두 거짓이라는 사실을 암시하려고
  b. 초감각적 지각이 통계학임을 암시하려고
  c. 카드 게임이 어떻게 진행되었는지 설명하려고
  d. 사람들이 정말로 초감각적 지각을 이용했던 것이 아니었음을 암시하려고
  e. 과학적인 연구 방법이 사용되었음을 암시하려고

구문해설

3행_ It may be used to gather information, to see objects located far away, or to control certain aspects of the environment.
⇒ to부정사의 부사적 용법 중 목적에 해당하며, to gather, to see, to control은 병렬관계를 이룬다.

6행_ there seems to be little hard data to confirm its existence
⇒ 문장 의미상 hard는 '확실한, 신뢰성 있는'이라는 뜻이다. to confirm은 명사 data를 수식하는 형용사적 용법으로 쓰였다.

9행_ J.B. Rhine, who invented the term *parapsychology* as a more scientific way of talking about ESP, was the first

to apply the principles of scientific analysis to this area of study.
⇒ 문장의 본동사는 was이며, 「the first+to do」는 '~을 처음하다'라는 뜻이다. 「apply A to B」는 'A를 B에 적용하다'라는 뜻이다.

15행_ The results of Rhine's tests suggested that some sort of ESP might have been used,
⇒ that은 접속사로 명사절을 이끌며, 동사 suggested의 목적어 역할을 한다. 「might+have+p.p.」는 과거의 불확실한 추측을 나타낸다.
⇒ 이밖에 「must+have+p.p.」는 과거에 대한 추정을 나타내어 '~이었음에 틀림없다', 「could+have+p.p.」는 과거의 사실에 반대되는 표현으로 '~할 수 있었을 텐데'의 뜻을 가지고 있다.

UNIT 13-1 | Empire State Building

Pre-reading Activity

102 stories

정답

1. c 2. d 3. a 4. e 5. a very distinctive spire

해석

엠파이어스테이트 빌딩은 뉴욕 시의 상징적 표상이다. 그것은 오랫동안 뉴욕 시에서 가장 높은 건물이었다. 세계 무역 센터인 유명한 쌍둥이 건물이 훨씬 높았지만, 쌍둥이 건물이 9월 11일 테러리스트들의 공격으로 파괴되면서 엠파이어스테이트 빌딩이 맨해튼의 스카이라인에서 최고의 자리를 다시 차지했다. 하지만 엠파이어스테이트 빌딩이 이렇게 항상 성공적이었던 것은 아니다.

1931년에 극적인 준공식에서 허버트 후버 대통령은 건물의 전기를 켜기 위해 워싱턴 D.C.에서 버튼을 눌렀다. 불행하게도 이는 대공황이 시작되는 시기에 일어났다. 당시에는 임대료를 낼 여력이 없어서 새로운 건물에 입주하는 데 관심을 보인 기업이 거의 없었다. 이는 건물 대부분이 오랫동안 빈 채로 남아 있어야 한다는 것을 의미했고, 이로 인해 엠파이어스테이트 빌딩은 빈 스테이트 빌딩(엠프티 스테이트 빌딩)이라는 별명을 얻었다. 옥상의 전망대는 사무실 임대 수익만큼이나 수익성이 좋은 것으로 판명되었다. 더 복잡한 이야기를 하자면 건물의 위치는 대중 교통수단을 이용하기에 조금 멀리 떨어져 있어서 접근하기에 편리하지 못했다.

엠파이어스테이트 빌딩의 꼭대기에는 매우 눈에 띄는 뾰족탑이 있어서 이 일대 지역의 다른 건물과는 완전히 달라 보였다.

이는 비행선의 도킹 스테이션으로 사용될 예정이었다. 1930년대에는 비행선이 교통수단으로 인기를 끌었다. 엠파이어스테이트 빌딩의 꼭대기 층은 공항처럼 설계되었다. 그 높이에서는 강한 바람이 불어서 도킹을 매우 불안전하게 만들었기 때문에 그 아이디어는 폐기되었다.

다행스럽게도 뉴욕이 미국의 사업과 금융 분야의 중심지로 성장하면서 맨해튼 지역 사무실에 대한 수요가 증가했다. 오늘날, 엠파이어스테이트 빌딩은 뉴욕 시의 스카이라인이라는 왕관에서도 상당히 사랑을 받는 보석이다.

◎ 해설

1 이 글의 주제는 무엇인가?
a. 맨해튼이 어떻게 발전했는지에 대한 설명
b. 뉴욕의 마천루의 역사에 대한 이야기
c. 엠파이어스테이트 빌딩의 역사에 대한 이야기
d. 마천루라는 단어의 기원을 설명
e. 엠파이어스테이트 빌딩과 다른 주요 마천루를 비교

2 빈칸에 들어갈 가장 적절한 말은 무엇인가?
a. 제출했다
b. 켰다
c. 커졌다
d. 판명되었다
e. 뒤집어졌다

3 다음 중 사실이 아닌 것은 무엇인가?
a. 엠파이어스테이트 빌딩은 도킹 스테이션으로 사용됐었다.
b. 엠파이어스테이트 빌딩은 현재 뉴욕에서 가장 높은 마천루이다.
c. 엠파이어스테이트 빌딩은 엠티 스테이트 빌딩이라는 별명이 있었다.
d. 세계 무역 센터였던 쌍둥이 빌딩이 뉴욕에서 가장 높은 건물이었다.
e. 경제 공황은 엠파이어스테이트 빌딩의 임대율에 영향을 주었다.

4 이 글에서 유추할 수 있는 것은 무엇인가?
a. 체펠린 비행선은 인기가 있는 교통수단이 되었다.
b. 엠파이어스테이트 빌딩을 건설한 사람들은 건물 완공 후에 파산했다.
c. 많은 건물이 엠파이어스테이트 빌딩과 유사한 모양으로 건설되었다.
d. 엠파이어스테이트 빌딩은 항상 뉴욕에서 가장 높은 마천루가 될 것이다.
e. 엠파이어스테이트 빌딩이 계획되었을 때, 사람들은 뉴욕 시의 바람의 패턴에 대해 아는 것이 거의 없었다.

5 "This"가 가리키는 것은 무엇인가?

◎ 구문해설

9행_ few businesses were interested in occupying the new building;

⇨ few는 부정적 용법으로 '거의 없는, 조금 밖에 없는'이란 뜻이며, 가산 명사를 수식한다. 또한 little도 부정적 용법으로 '조금밖에 없는, 거의 없는'이란 뜻이며 불가산 명사를 수식한다.

11행_ The rooftop observation deck turned out to be as profitable as renting offices.

⇨ 「turn out + to부정사」는 '~으로 판명되다'라는 뜻이다.

☆ He turned out to be a thief. (그는 도둑으로 판명되었다.)

14행_ On top of the Empire State Building, there is a very distinctive spire, making it quite different from any other building in the area.

⇨ making it quite different from any other building in the area은 분사구문으로 의미상의 주어는 a very distinctive spire이다. 대명사 it은 the Empire State Building을 나타낸다.

UNIT 13-2 Petronas Twin Towers

◎ 정답

1. c   2. a   3. e   4. d   5. c

◎ 해석

말레이시아의 수도 쿠알라룸푸르에 있는 페트로나스 트윈 타워는 세계에서 가장 높은 건물이었다. 건물은 1998년에 완공되었고 다음 6년 동안 타이베이 101이 문을 열 때까지 세계에서 가장 높은 건물이라는 영예도 얻었다.

건축가 시저 펠리가 설계한 타워는 강철이 아닌 철근 콘크리트로 지어졌다는 점에서 특이하다. 강철을 수입하는 비용이 너무 비싸서 실용적이지 않았다. 콘크리트 건물은 강철로 지어진 건물보다 덜 흔들린다는 또 다른 장점이 있다. 쿠알라룸푸르 아래에 있는 기반암의 두께에 더하여 건물의 막대한 무게는 세계에서 가장 깊은 120미터라는 기반이 필요하다는 뜻이 된다.

트윈 타워는 말레이시아를 위한 개발 프로그램의 걸작품이 될 것이었다. 제1타워는 말레이시아 국유 회사인 페트로나스가 사용한다. 제2타워는 로이터, IBM, 알자지라, 보잉사 등과 같은 기업체가 임대해 있는 상업용 사무실 건물로 사용된다. 타워의 아래쪽에는 쿠알라룸푸르 시티 센터로 수리아 KLCC라 불리는 6층짜리 고급 쇼핑몰이 있다. 이 쇼핑몰은 17에이커에 달하는 공원으로 둘러싸여 있다. 지하에는 쿠알라룸푸르의 새 지하철 노선 중 하나가 지나는 역이 있다.

방문객들은 41층과 42층에서 두 타워를 연결하는 구름다리까지 올라갈 수 있다. 이는 세계에서 가장 높은 이 층짜리 다리이다. 페트로나스에 종사하는 사람들이나 제2타워에 입주해 있는 회사에서 일하는 사람들만이 더 높은 층에 올라갈 수 있다. 더욱이 하루에 1,700명만이 구름다리를 방문할 수 있다. 입장권은 선착순으로 배분된다. 건축학적으로 세계에서 가장 중요한 건물의 한 곳에서 경관을 보고 싶다면 아침에 일찍 도착하도록 계획을 세워라.

○ 해설

1 이 글의 제목과 바꿔 쓸 수 있는 가장 적절한 것은 무엇인가?

　a. 타이베이 101
　b. 세상에서 가장 높은 건물들
　c. 쿠알라룸푸르의 쌍둥이 건물
　d. 콘크리트 건축의 기적
　e. 페트로나스 트윈 타워에 입주한 회사들

2 "practical"의 뜻에 가장 가까운 단어는 무엇인가?

　a. 실용적인
　b. 자격 있는
　c. 불가능한
　d. 전문적인
　e. 정교한

3 빈칸에 들어갈 가장 적절한 말은 무엇인가?

　a. 인터넷으로 예약을 해라.
　b. 들어갈 때 신분증을 보여 줘라.
　c. 트윈 타워에 입주한 회사에 일자리를 얻어라.
　d. 트윈 타워에 큰돈을 기부하라.
　e. 아침 일찍 도착하도록 계획을 세워라.

4 빈칸에 들어갈 가장 적절한 말은 무엇인가?

> 페트로나스 트윈 타워는 타이베이 101이 이 트윈 타워를 <u>능가하기 전</u>까지 세계에서 가장 높은 건물이었다.

　a. 동안, 짓는
　b. 까지, 창조하기
　c. 동안, 항복하는
　d. 전까지, 능가하기
　e. 동안, 변형하는

5 이 글의 목적은 무엇인가?

　a. 콘크리트 건축의 이점에 대해 설명하려고
　b. 쿠알라룸푸르의 발전에 대해 이야기하려고
　c. 페트로나스 타워의 개관을 이야기하려고
　d. 말레이시아의 건축 방법을 독자들에게 소개하려고
　e. 페트로나스 트윈 타워와 타이베이 101을 비교하려고

○ 구문해설

5행_ The towers, which were designed by the architect César Pelli, are unusual in that they are built of reinforced concrete, not steel.

⇒ 주어는 The towers이며, 본동사는 are이다. in that은 '~라는 점에서'라는 의미를 가지고 있다.

8행_ The buildings' enormous weight, coupled with the depth of the bedrock below that part of Kuala Lumpur, meant that a very deep—the world's deepest, at 120 meters—foundation was needed.

⇒ 주어는 The buildings' enormous weight이며 본동사는 meant이다. coupled with는 '~와 더불어'라는 의미이며, that은 접속사로 명사절을 이끌어 동사 meant의 목적어 역할을 한다.

18행_ Visitors may go as high as the skybridge that connects the two towers at the 41st and 42nd floors.

⇒ 조동사 may는 '~할 수 있다'는 가능의 의미이며, that은 주격 관계대명사로 선행사는 the skybridge이다.

21행_ Only people who work for Petronas or one of the companies in Tower 2 are permitted to go to the higher floors.

⇒ who는 주격 관계대명사로 형용사절을 이끌어 주어 people를 수식하며, 본동사는 are이다. 「be permitted to+동사원형」은 '~하는 것을 허락 받다'의 뜻이다.

UNIT 14-1　The Search for the Dalai Lama

○ Pre-reading Activity

plateau, roof, administered

○ 정답

1. d　2. b　3. e　4. b　5. He was taken away from the parents and brought back to the monastery to be raised by the monks.

○ 해석

티베트의 오래된 관습에 따르면 새로운 종교 및 정치 지도자는 이전 지도자가 사망할 때마다 태어난다. 티베트의 리더는 예외 없이 달라이 라마로 불리는 승려이다. 1933년에 13대 달라이 라마가 사망했을 때, 승려와 정부 관리가 달라이 라마의 환생이라고 믿는 아기를 찾기 시작했다. 과거에 이 과정은 대개 2년에서 3년이 걸렸지만 14대 달라이 라마를 찾는 데는 4년이 걸렸다.

수색 팀은 고대 상징과 표시된 정보를 따라간다. 사망한 달라이 라마의 머리가 향하는 방향이 수색에 관련된 한 가지 요소였다. 이와 더불어 수색 팀의 한 구성원이 외딴 암도(Amdo) 지역의 환상을 보았다. 이는 중요한 현상으로 여기는데, 왜냐하면 호수 옆의 작은 오두막의 형상이 매우 자세히 보였기 때문이

다. 오랜 수색 끝에 호수를 찾았고, 오두막을 발견했다. 수색 팀 중 한 명이 이전 달라이 라마의 가장 친한 친구였다. 그가 집으로 걸어 들어갔고, 아이가 그를 보았을 때 아이의 눈에서 그를 알아보는 눈빛을 느낄 수 있었다. 그 사람이 많은 물건을 가지고 가서 아이에게 보여 주었고, 아이는 13대 달라이 라마의 물건들을 골라 낼 수 있었다. 그는 부모에게서 떨어져 승려의 손에 양육되도록 수도원으로 보내졌다. 승려들은 1940년 겨울에 달라이 라마를 찾았다는 공식적인 발표를 했다. 그때 이후로 달라이 라마는 티베트 사람들의 지도자로서만이 아니라 전 세계 사람들의 정신적인 지도자로 폭넓은 존경을 받고 있다.

◉ 해설

1 이 글의 주제는 무엇인가?
  a. 티베트의 오래된 미신
  b. 티베트의 정치적 분쟁
  c. 티베트 지도자의 죽음
  d. 티베트 지도자의 선정
  e. 달라이 라마를 찾는 무리

2 "he"가 가리키는 것은 무엇인가?
  a. 13대 달라이 라마
  b. 14대 달라이 라마
  c. 아이의 부모 중 한 명
  d. 달라이 라마를 찾는 무리 중 한 명
  e. 13대 달라이 라마의 가장 친한 친구

3 "proclamation"의 뜻에 가장 가까운 단어는 무엇인가?
  a. 규칙
  b. 행사
  c. 적법성
  d. 여흥
  e. 발표

4 빈칸에 들어갈 가장 적절한 말은 무엇인가?

> 수색 팀은 죽은 달라이 라마로부터 그의 계승자를 찾을 수 있는 단서를 발견했다. 수색 팀이 14대 달라이 라마를 발견하고 사원으로 데려갔다.

  a. 표시, 파트너, 선출했다
  b. 단서, 계승자, 데려갔다
  c. 섬광, 우상, 데려왔다
  d. 힌트, 선임자, 데려갔다
  e. 허가, 계승자, 걸어갔다

5 14대 달라이 라마가 발견된 후에, 그에게 무슨 일이 일어났는가?

◉ 구문해설

5행_ a group of monks and government officials began the search for the baby they believed to be his reincarnation
⇨ the baby와 they 사이에 목적격 관계대명사가 생략되었다.

11행_ The direction that the deceased Dalai Lama's head was facing was one factor involved in the search.
⇨ that은 목적격 관계대명사로 형용사절을 이끌어 주어 the direction을 수식하고 있으며, 본동사는 두 번째 was이다.

19행_ he was able to choose the ones that belonged to the 13th Dalai Lama
⇨ ones는 부정대명사로 items를 대신해 쓰였으며, that은 주격 관계대명사로 선행사는 the ones이다.

20행_ He was taken away from the parents and brought back to the monastery to be raised by the monks.
⇨ '부모로부터 떨어져 수도원으로 보내졌다'는 뜻으로 수동태로 쓰인 것에 유의하자. to be raised는 to부정사의 부사적 용법 중 목적을 나타내어 '양육되어지기 위해'라고 해석한다.

22행_ Since then, the Dalai Lama has earned widespread admiration, not just as the leader of the Tibetan people but as a spiritual leader to people around the world.
⇨ 「not just[only, merely, simply] ~ but (also.)」는 '~ 뿐만 아니라 …도 (또한)'이라는 의미이다.

UNIT 14-2 The Papal Conclave

◉ Pre-reading Activity
1. T   2. T   3. F   4. F

◉ 정답
1. a   2. a   3. d   4. e   5. It is a special meeting of all the cardinals below the age of 80 held in the Vatican to elect the pope.

◉ 해석
교황은 가톨릭교회의 지도자이고, 새로운 교황을 선출할 때에는 매우 독특한 선거가 진행된다. 80세 이하인 모든 추기경의 특별 모임인 교황 선출 콘클라베가 바티칸에서 열린다. 이 콘클라베는 1천 년 이상이 된, 세계에서 가장 오래된 지도자 선출 과정이다.
교황 선출 콘클라베가 설립되기 전에는 성직자와 로마 시민들이 교황을 선출하곤 했다. 하지만 1268년에서 1271년 사이에는 극심한 정치적 간섭 때문에 교황이 선출되지 못했다. 이에 따른 혼란을 겪으면서 결정권을 소유한 로마 가톨릭교회 위원회는 선출 과정 동안 교황 선출 콘클라베의 구성원들을 가둬 놓겠다고 선언하기에 이르렀다! 그들은 새로운 교황이 선출되기까지는 글자 그대로 자리를 뜰 수 없다. 몸이 아픈 추기경은 자리를 뜰 수 있지만 그런 전통은 오늘날까지 계속되고 있다.

콘클라베는 며칠에 걸쳐 기도하고 논의하고 투표하는 과정을 거친다. 교황 후보자 명단이 발표되고 매체에서 토론되는 경우가 종종 있기는 하지만, 추기경들은 교황에 선출되려고 선거운동을 하지는 않는다. 투표에는 세 가지 단계가 있는데, 그것은 궁극적으로 다음 교황이 될 한 사람으로 후보자의 선택을 좁혀나가는 것이다. 언제나 상당한 의견 차이가 있지만, 다음 교황은 3분의 2라는 과반수 찬성에 의해 선출되어야 한다. 선택이 일단 이뤄지고 나면 로마 전체에 종이 울리고 하얀 연기 신호가 피어오른다.

콘클라베 동안에는 비공개에 대한 매우 엄격한 규칙이 적용된다. 기자는 내부에 들어갈 수 없고, 현 교황인 베네딕토 16세를 선출하는 동안에는 콘클라베가 진행되는 회의실도 도청 장치를 찾으려고 검사했다. 콘클라베 과정을 바꾸자는 제안이 있었다. 콘클라베는 변화가 생기든 아니든 간에 매우 흥미로운 구경거리임에는 틀림없다.

해설

1 이 글의 주제는 무엇인가?
   a. 교황 선출
   b. 추기경의 선정
   c. 추기경의 비밀회의
   d. 종교와 정치 사이의 분쟁
   e. 로마 가톨릭 교회의 역사

2 "fiasco"의 뜻에 가장 가까운 단어는 무엇인가?
   a. 대혼란
   b. 회기
   c. 생략
   d. 비밀회의
   e. 선택

3 다음 중 사실인 것은 무엇인가?
   a. 가장 유력한 교황 후보들은 정치인처럼 선거 유세를 한다.
   b. 교황은 만장일치로 선출되어야 한다.
   c. 오래 전에는 로마 정부가 새 교황을 임명했다.
   d. 예전에는 성직자와 로마 시민들이 직접 교황을 선출했다.
   e. 현 교황이 선출된 회의 때 어떤 기자가 마이크를 숨겨서 도청했다.

4 글쓴이가 전자 도청 장치를 언급한 이유는 무엇인가?
   a. 이야기의 흥미를 떨어뜨리려고
   b. 스파이 스릴러 영화를 연상시키려고
   c. 언론이 선거 과정에 준 영향을 보여 주려고
   d. 비밀회의에 참여한 추기경 중 몇 명이 스파이임을 암시하려고
   e. 교황을 선출하는 비밀회의에 대한 사람들의 관심이 얼마나 큰지 알려 주려고

5 "papal conclave"는 무엇인가?

구문해설

5행_ the clergy and the people of Rome used to elect the pope
⇨ 「used to+동사원형」은 과거의 습관적인 규칙을 나타내어 '~하곤 했다'라는 의미이다.

7행_ The resulting fiasco led the ruling Council of the Roman Catholic Church to decree that the members of the papal conclave had to be locked in during the selection process!
⇨ that은 접속사로 명사절을 이끌고 있으며, decree와 동격을 나타낸다.

14행_ There are three phases of voting, which eventually narrow down the choice of candidates to the one meant to be the next pope.
⇨ which는 주격 관계대명사로 선행사는 three phases of voting이다. 과거분사 meant는 부정대명사 one을 후치 수식하고 있다.

17행_ Once the selection has been made, bells ring throughout Rome and a white smoke signal is given.
⇨ once는 접속사로 '일단 ~하면'이란 의미이다. 이밖에 once는 부사 및 명사로도 자주 쓰인다.
once a day 하루에 한 번, once in a while 때때로, at once 즉시

UNIT 15-1 Jean-Paul Gaultier

정답

1. b   2. a   3. c   4. a   5. b

해석

장폴 고띠에는 현대 패션계에서 가장 영향력 있는 디자이너 중 한 사람이다. 1952년에 파리의 남부 근교에서 출생한 고띠에는 실제로 디자이너로서 정식 교육을 받은 적이 없다. 그는 혼자서 패션 스케치를 그리기 시작했다. 1970년대 초에 전설적인 디자이너 피에르 가르뎅이 그의 스케치 일부를 보고 매우 깊은 인상을 받아서 고띠에를 즉시 고용했다.

고띠에는 1976년에 첫 단독 의상 발표회로 데뷔를 했다. 하지만 고띠에를 유명하게 만든 대담하고 도발적인 디자인은 1981년까지 나타나지 않았다. 그는 곧 프랑스 패션계의 무서운 아이 또는 악동으로 인정을 받았다. 미국인들은 주로 그가 마돈나의 의상을 디자인하기 시작했던 1990년대 초반이 되어서야 비로

소 그를 알기 시작했다. 고띠에가 디자인한 '콘 브라'로 알려진 뷔스티에(몸에 꼭 끼고 소매와 어깨 끈이 없는 여성 웃옷 또는 브래지어)는 전 세계적으로 뉴스거리가 되었다. 사람들은 깜짝 놀라면서도 호기심을 보였고 고띠에는 국제적인 유명 인사가 되었다.

고띠에는 패션 산업계의 관습에 지속적으로 도전했다. 그의 디자인은 장난스럽고 틀에 얽매이지 않고 종종 충격적이었다. 그의 웃은 파리의 빈민가에서 볼 수 있는 거리 패션을 바탕으로 하는 경우가 많았다. 그는 아이디어와 영감을 찾으면서 도시의 중고 시장과 재고 판매 시장에서 정기적으로 쇼핑하였다. 또한 그는 모델에 관한 업계의 기대치에 도전하기를 좋아했다. 자신의 패션쇼에서 그는 매우 날씬하고 예쁜 젊은 남녀를 고용하지 않고 때로 몸집이 큰 여성, 나이 든 남성, 커다란 문신을 한 사람들을 고용했다. 그전에는 어떤 디자이너도 그토록 대담하게 업계의 관습에 도전하지 않았는데, 사람들은 그런 도전을 좋아했다.

고띠에는 주요 영화와 음악 콘서트를 위한 의상을 디자인했고, 그의 패션은 파리에서 가장 유명한 사람들 사이에 지속적으로 존재했다. 그는 분명히 생존해 있는 디자이너 가운데 가장 중요한 인물 중 한 사람이다.

○ 해설

1 이 글의 주제는 무엇인가?
   a. 패션 디자이너가 되는 방법
   b. 장폴 고띠에의 패션 경력
   c. 파리에서의 장폴 고띠에의 사업
   d. 피에르 가르댕이 장폴 고띠에에게 준 영향
   e. 프랑스 패션과 미국 패션의 비교

2 "slender"의 뜻에 가장 가까운 단어는 무엇인가?
   a. 날씬한
   b. 작은
   c. 통통한
   d. 기울은
   e. 아름다운

3 이 글에서 유추할 수 있는 것은 무엇인가?
   a. 장폴 고띠에는 건장한 여자를 좋아한다.
   b. 고띠에는 지극히 평범하고 전통적인 옷을 디자인한다.
   c. 디자이너들은 대개 날씬하고 아름다운 모델을 원한다.
   d. 과거에는 많은 패션 디자이너들이 정규 교육을 거의 받지 못했다.
   e. 고띠에는 어렸을 때 파리의 빈민가에서 살았다.

4 빈칸에 들어갈 가장 적절한 말은 무엇인가?
   a. 논쟁의 여지없이
   b. 특별하게
   c. 설명할 수 없게
   d. 무의식적으로

   e. 독립적으로

5 이 글의 목적은 무엇인가?
   a. 프랑스 패션에 대한 개관을 알려 주려고
   b. 장폴 고띠에의 경력을 설명하려고
   c. 프랑스 디자인 경향의 발전에 대해 논의하려고
   d. 장폴 고띠에와 피에르 가르댕을 비교하려고
   e. 고띠에와 다른 중요한 패션 디자이너들을 비교하려고

○ 구문해설

7행_ the daring and provocative designs Gaultier became known for did not appear until 1981
⇨ designs와 Gaultier 사이에 목적격 관계대명사가 생략되었다고 생각하면 문장 구조를 쉽게 이해할 수 있다.

10행_ The bustier that Gaultier designed, featuring what came to be known as the "cone bra," made news all over the world.
⇨ that은 목적격 관계대명사로 주어 the bustier를 수식하는 형용사절을 이끌고 있으며, featuring what came to be known as the "cone bra"는 분사구문으로 의미상의 주어는 The bustier이다. 본동사는 made이다.

15행_ His clothes were often based on street wear found in the rough neighborhoods of Paris,
⇨ be based on은 '~에 기초를 두다'라는 뜻이다. 과거분사 found가 명사 street wear를 후치 수식하고 있다.

16행_ he became a regular shopper at the capital's second-hand bazaars and rummage sales, looking for ideas and inspiration
⇨ looking for ideas and inspiration은 분사구문으로 의미상의 주어는 he다.

UNIT 15-2 Coco Chanel

○ Pre-reading Activity

1. F   2. T   3. T

○ 정답

1. a   2. c   3. d   4. b   5. a

○ 해석

샤넬의 유명한 디자인 하우스를 세운 코코 샤넬은 1883년에 프랑스 서부의 한 마을에서 태어났다. 그녀는 여섯 형제 중 한 명으로, 가난한 가정에서 출생했다. 열두 살 때 어머니께서 돌

아가셨고 아버지는 가족을 떠났다. 그녀와 살아 남은 네 명의 형제들은 보육원으로 보내졌다. 코코는 10대에 재봉사 훈련을 받았고 그녀의 여성 친척들 몇 명이 그녀에게 고급 재봉 기술을 가르쳐 주었다.

그녀는 열여덟 살에 보육원을 떠나서 한 재봉사 밑에서 일하기 시작했다. 그녀는 그리 오래지 않아 파리 출신의 한 부유한 남성을 만나는 행운을 누렸다. 그는 그녀에게 좋은 옷과 보석을 사주었고, 이를 계기로 그녀는 손수 디자인을 하고 싶다는 마음을 먹게 되었다. 그녀는 여성용 모자를 디자인하기 시작했는데 이 모자가 곧 인기를 끌게 되었다. 그녀는 이 첫 성공을 이용해서 파리로 이전하고 나서 사업을 확장해서 레인코트와 재킷을 포함시켰다. 그녀의 옷은 프랑스 연극 여배우들과 사교계 여성들의 사랑을 받았지만, 제1차와 제2차 세계 대전이라는 큰 장애물에 직면했다.

코코는 패션에서 많은 중요한 유행 스타일을 확립하는 것에 대한 책임을 졌다. 그녀의 디자인은 단순함과 편안함에 초점을 두었으며, 이것은 이전에 여성들이 착용했던 꽉 끼고, 조이는 옷들과 커다란 변화이다. 그녀의 목표는 여성들에게 해방감을 부여하는 것이었다. 그녀는 시간을 초월한 모습을 창출하기 위해 새로운 시즌마다 옷을 바꾸지 않고 기본적인 디자인을 매우 조금씩 수정하는 쪽으로 했다. 결과적으로 많은 샤넬 디자인은 해를 거듭해도 지속적으로 좋아 보인다. 또한 그녀의 유명한 향수인 샤넬 NO. 5는 디자이너의 이름을 딴 최초의 향수였다. 그녀는 패션계에 미친 영향력이 너무나 커서 〈타임〉지가 선정한 20세기의 가장 영향력 있는 사람 100위의 명단에 디자이너로 유일하게 선정되었다.

○ 해설

1 두 번째 문단의 주제는 무엇인가?
   a. 샤넬의 경력의 시작
   b. 영향력 있는 프랑스 디자이너
   c. 샤넬의 불우한 어린 시절
   d. 파리에서의 샤넬의 인기
   e. 세계 대전이 샤넬의 디자인에 미친 영향

2 "confining"의 뜻에 가장 가까운 단어는 무엇인가?
   a. 금속의
   b. 상쾌한
   c. 꽉 조이는
   d. 비싼
   e. 편안한

3 다음 중 사실이 아닌 것은 무엇인가?
   a. 코코 샤넬의 형제자매 중 한 명이 죽었다.
   b. 코코 샤넬의 가족은 매우 가난했다.
   c. 샤넬이 디자인 한 첫 번째 패션 품목은 모자였다.

   d. 코코 샤넬의 사업은 세계 대전의 영향을 받지 않았다.
   e. 코코 샤넬은 젊었을 때 부유한 애인이 있었다.

4 빈칸에 들어갈 가장 적절한 말은 무엇인가?
   a. 돈을 절약하기
   b. 시간을 초월한 모습을 창출하기
   c. 연극배우들에게 깊은 인상을 주기
   d. 사람들을 젊어 보이게 하기
   e. 값이 나가 보이는 옷을 만들기

5 샤넬의 옷이 세월이 흘러도 계속 좋아 보이는 이유는 무엇인가?
   a. 샤넬의 옷은 해가 바뀌어도 변화가 거의 없으며, 디자인이 간결하다.
   b. 고급 의류를 만드는 회사는 옷의 디자인을 매년 바꾼다.
   c. 패션 디자이너들에게 있어서 대중의 취향을 예측하는 것은 쉬운 일이다.
   d. 샤넬의 옷은 많은 다른 디자이너들의 옷을 모방한 것이다.
   e. 샤넬의 옷은 매년 비싸지고 있다.

○ 구문해설

9행_ this inspired her to begin designing on her own
⇒ 「inspire+목적어+to부정사」의 문장 구조를 알아두자.

10행_ She started with women's hats, **which** quickly became popular,
⇒ which는 관계대명사의 계속적 용법으로 and they로 바꿔 쓸 수 있다.

16행_ Her designs focused on simplicity and comfort, a big change from the tight, confining clothes women had previously worn.
⇒ clothes와 women 사이에 목적격 관계대명사가 생략되었다.

24행_ Her impact on the fashion world was so great that she was the only designer chosen among TIME Magazine's list of the most 100 most influential people of the 20th century.
⇒ 「so ~ that …」은 '너무 ~해서 …하다'라는 뜻이며, 과거분사 chosen과 designer 사이에 「관계대명사+be동사」가 생략되었다고 생각하면 문장 구조를 쉽게 이해할 수 있다.

◎ 정답

1. e   2. d   3. b   4. e   5. c

◎ 해석

폴 왓슨과 그의 참모들, 자원봉사자 단체는 연구라는 명목으로 고래를 사냥하는 일본 선박을 찾아서 저지시키기 위한 운동을 거의 매년 겨울 벌여 왔다. 왓슨은 '스티브 어윈'이라는 배의 선장이다. 왓슨과 그의 선원들은 멸종 위기에 처한 바다 생물을 구하기 위해 헌신하고 있다. 몸집이 더 큰 고래의 많은 종은 1986년에 상업용 고래잡이 금지가 발표되기 전까지 그 수가 심각하게 감소했다. 그리고 비록 일부 종들이 그때 이후로 현저하게 복구되고 있지만, 북방흑고래 같은 기타 고래들은 상당히 심각한 멸종 위기에 놓여 있다.

2009년 2월에 자연보호론자인 선장이 이렇게 언급했다. "우리의 선박 '스티브 어윈'은 '고래 사망의 주역'인 일본 고래잡이 어선 '니신마루'를 열두 시간째 쫓아가고 있다. 우리는 매시간 이 잔인한 고래잡이 기계이자 산업주의에 물든 물위에 떠다니는 고래 도살장에 가까이 다가가고 있다." 일본인들은 '과학을 위한 고래잡이'라는 허점을 이용해서 지난 20년 이상 계속해서 고래를 죽이고 있다. 왓슨은 실질적인 목적은 연구가 아니라고 주장한다. 일부 사람들은 고래 고기가 결국 식료품점의 판매대 위에 놓이게 될 것이라고 말한다.

'스티브 어윈'과 고래잡이 선박 사이의 대립으로 신문에 기사가 크게 날 만큼 심각한 충돌이 두 번 발생했다. 고래잡이 선박은 음파를 일으키는 불법 무기를 사용했다는 이유로 기소되었다. 이 때문에 왓슨이 이끄는 선원들은 어지러움을 느끼고 방향 감각을 상실하고 귀와 눈에 손상을 입었을지도 모른다. 또한 일본인 고래잡이 선원들은 '스티브 어윈'의 선원들을 향해서 강력한 물대포를 쏘았다. 이에 상응하여 일본 선원들은 선박을 충돌하게 했다는 이유로 '스티브 어윈'을 기소했다.

이 문제와 관련된 양측 사람들의 태도는 위험하고 논쟁의 여지가 있다. 제기해야 할 쟁점은 불법 고래잡이 조업으로 추정되는 행위에 대항한 폭력이 정당화되는지 여부이다.

◎ 해설

1 이 글의 주제는 무엇인가?
   a. 위대한 환경보호론자 '스티브 어윈'
   b. 일본 크루즈 배 '니신 마루'
   c. 고래잡이가 환경에 끼친 해악
   d. 미국과 일본의 환경 논쟁
   e. '스티브 어윈'선의 선원들의 고래잡이 반대 운동

2 "depleted"의 뜻에 가장 가까운 단어는 무엇인가?
   a. 주도했다
   b. 세 배가 됐다
   c. 합쳤다
   d. 감소했다
   e. 확장했다

3 다음 중 사실인 것은 무엇인가?
   a. 일본 요리에는 고래 고기가 포함되지 않는다.
   b. 1986년 이후로 상업적인 고래잡이가 금지되었다.
   c. '스티브 어윈'선의 선원은 항상 비폭력적으로 행동했다.
   d. '스티브 어윈'선의 선원은 환경에 심각한 해를 가한 것에 대한 책임이 있다.
   e. '니신 마루'의 선원은 불법적인 무기를 사용하지 않았을 것이다.

4 빈칸에 들어갈 가장 적절한 말은 무엇인가?

> 상업적인 고래잡이가 금지된 이후에도 일본사람들은 과학적인 연구라고 <u>주장하면서</u> 고래 사냥을 <u>계속할</u> 수 있었다.

   a. 중지할, 주장하면서
   b. 요구할, 부인하면서
   c. 저항할, 주장하면서
   d. 계속할, 부인하면서
   e. 계속할, 주장하면서

5 글쓴이가 '스티브 어윈'선과 일본 고래잡이배의 충돌을 언급한 이유는 무엇인가?
   a. 법을 고쳐야 함을 알려 주려고
   b. 고래 고기가 풍미 있고 맛있다는 것을 암시하려고
   c. 양편이 모두 법에 저촉되는 행동을 하고 있음을 알려 주려고
   d. '스티브 어윈'선의 선원이 체포되어야 한다는 것을 암시하려고
   e. 일본사람들이 '스티브 어윈'선의 선원들보다 나쁘다는 것을 암시하려고

◎ 구문해설

1행_ Paul Watson and his group of staff and volunteers have engaged in a campaign almost every winter <u>to find and stop</u> Japanese ships <u>that</u> hunt whales in the name of research.

⇒ to find and stop은 to부정사의 부사적 용법 중 목적을 나타내고 있다. that 은 주격 관계대명사로, 선행사는 Japanese ships이다.

6행_ And although some species <u>have shown</u> significant recovery since then, others <u>like</u> the Northern Right Whale remain critically endangered.

⇒ have shown은 현재완료의 계속적 용법을 나타내고 있다. like는 전치사로 '~ 같은, ~처럼' 등의 뜻을 가지고 있다.

16행_ Confrontations between the *Steve Irwin* and the whaling fleet have resulted in <u>two collisions</u> serious enough to make the headlines.

⇒ two collisions와 serious 사이에 「관계대명사+be동사」가 생략되었다.

24행_ The question that needs to be asked is whether violence against alleged illegal whaling operations is justified.

⇨ that은 주격 관계대명사로 형용사절을 이끌어 주어 The question을 수식하며, 본동사는 is이다. 접속사 whether는 명사절을 이끌어 주격보어 역할을 한다.

UNIT 16-2 The Great Pacific Garbage Patch

◉ 정답

1. b   2. a   3. b   4. e   5. **There is little wind across the center of the North Pacific Gyre.**

◉ 해석

배를 타고 태평양을 가로지른다고 상상해 보라. 하루는 바다를 내다보다가 수평선까지 죽 뻗어 있는 쓰레기 층을 본다. 이런 이야기는 악몽처럼 들릴지 모르지만 불행하게도 존재한다. 거대한 태평양 쓰레기 더미로 알려져 있고, 물이 심각하게 오염되어 있는 이 지역은 최소한 프랑스 면적의 두 배이거나 어쩌면 이보다 훨씬 넓은 면적을 차지하고 있을 것이다. 하지만, 이것이 어떻게 생겨났고 이에 대해 어떤 조치를 취할 수 있을까?

북태평양 환류는 태평양의 북부 지역에서 시계 방향으로 선회하는 해류이다. 이 해류는 미국의 서해안과 필리핀, 일본을 지난다. 이 나라들과 다른 나라에서 방출되는 쓰레기가 바다로 휩쓸려 나가 중앙에 있는 쓰레기 더미에 추가된다. 이 중앙 지역을 가로지르는 바람이 거의 없어서 대부분의 쓰레기는 소용돌이치는 물에 의해 그곳에 갇히게 된다.

쓰레기의 약 80%는 육지에서 오고, 또 다른 20%는 지나가는 선박에서 떨어진다고 알려져 있다. 대부분이 플라스틱인 이 쓰레기는 병, 음식 포장재, 버려진 포장 재료, 기타 쓰레기로 이뤄져 있다. 시간이 흐르면서 햇빛이 플라스틱을 더욱 작은 조각으로 분해한다. 플라스틱 조각이 충분히 작아지면 플랑크톤, 물고기, 바닷새, 기타 유기체에 의해 소비된다. 이런 플라스틱은 그들의 몸에 축적되어 그들을 병이 들게 하거나 죽인다. 또한 오염은 사람을 포함해서 먹이 사슬의 더 높은 단계에 있는 동물에게 영향을 미친다.

하지만 희망은 있다. 쓰레기 더미를 연구하고 물고기는 포획하지 않으면서 플라스틱을 청소할 수 있는 특수한 그물을 끌 수 있는 선박을 보내기 위해 가이세이 프로젝트라는 계획이 개발되고 있다. 이 계획은 유엔과 일부 미국 대학, 다수의 재단과 사기업의 지원을 받고 있다. 쓰레기는 재활용될 것이고 따라서 매우 심각한 환경적 문제가 긍정적으로 활용될 것이다.

◉ 해설

1 이 글의 제목과 바꿔 쓸 수 있는 가장 적절한 것은 무엇인가?
- **a.** 바다를 깨끗하게 하기 위한 방법
- **b.** 대양의 쓰레기 소용돌이
- **c.** 프랑스의 쓰레기 문제
- **d.** 태평양에서 가장 낚시하기 좋은 장소
- **e.** 지나다니는 배에서 버려진 쓰레기

2 "deploy"의 뜻에 가장 가까운 단어는 무엇인가?
- **a.** 배치하다
- **b.** 고갈시키다
- **c.** 탐험하다
- **d.** 보류하다
- **e.** 생산하다

3 쓰레기 소용돌이 현상에 대한 글쓴이는 태도는 어떠한가?
- **a.** 부정적인
- **b.** 희망적인
- **c.** 희망이 없는
- **d.** 절망적인
- **e.** 염세적인

4 이 글의 목적은 무엇인가?
- **a.** 독자들을 겁주려고
- **b.** 독자들이 생선을 섭취하는 것을 그만두게 하려고
- **c.** 전 세계적인 쓰레기 문제에 대해 이야기하려고
- **d.** 독자들의 식습관을 바꾸려고
- **e.** 독자들에게 해양 쓰레기 문제를 인식시키려고

5 북태평양 소용돌이의 중심 부분에 쓰레기 대부분이 갇혀 있는 이유는 무엇인가?

◉ 구문해설

1행_ One day you look out at the water and see a layer of garbage that extends all the way to the horizon.

⇨ that은 주격 관계대명사로 선행사는 a layer이다.

9행_ Garbage from these countries and others is swept out to sea and added to the mass of waste in the center.

⇨ 주어는 Garbage이며 is swept와 (is) added의 수동형 문장이다.

20행_ A plan called *Project Kaisei* has been developed to study the garbage patch and deploy a fleet of ships dragging special nets to clean up the plastic without catching fish.

⇨ called는 과거분사로 명사 plan을 후치 수식하고 있으며, to study와 deploy는 to부정사의 부사적 용법에 목적에 해당된다. 현재분사 dragging은 ships를 후치 수식하고 있다.

Unit Review **Answers**

UNIT 1

A-1 1. prosperous 2. lax 3. access 4. heartless 5. harmful
A-2 1. b 2. c 3. a 4. c 5. d
A-3 1. alternative 2. Poverty 3. stereotype 4. soot 5. founder
B-1 1. mutually exclusive 2. as a result 3. in the field of 4. No matter what
B-2 1. make a buck 2. sprung up 3. get ahead 4. are looking into
C   enacted, poverty, unprecedented, potential, entrepreneurs, develop, borrow, social

UNIT 2

A-1 1. massacre 2. return 3. outrage 4. independence 5. unjust
A-2 1. b 2. a 3. d 4. c 5. d
A-3 1. flexible 2. oppose 3. steady 4. assassinate 5. threatened
B-1 1. under the law 2. By this time 3. Once again 4. Upon her return
B-2 1. called for 2. cooperate with 3. rips apart 4. was related to
C   admiration, figure, violence, resistance, gave up, rose, won, reunited, accomplished

UNIT 3

A-1 1. leftovers 2. gross 3. citrus 4. viable 5. alternative
A-2 1. c 2. d 3. a 4. d 5. b
A-3 1. unrecognizable 2. harvested 3. appropriate 4. essentially 5. moist
B-1 1. in the near future 2. In most cases 3. Now that 4. Best of all
B-2 1. come up with 2. keep, in mind 3. broke down 4. tossed, out
C   recycling, broken down, fertilizer, garbage, alternative, run on, dependence, cut down

UNIT 4

A-1 1. notify 2. seek 3. spokesperson 4. relieved 5. poise
A-2 1. c 2. d 3. a 4. c 5. d
A-3 1. risk 2. sensible 3. investigator 4. ordeal 5. precaution
B-1 1. in the vicinity 2. a great deal of 3. on holiday 4. nothing but
B-2 1. show up 2. make sure 3. takes off 4. ended up
C   stranded, prepared, supplies, rescuers, decision, take-off, turn back, prevented

UNIT 5

A-1 1. attempt 2. decline 3. extinct 4. discovery 5. allow
A-2 1. d 2. b 3. d 4. b 5. b
A-3 1. particularly 2. immunity 3. native 4. overthrow 5. presence
B-1 1. as well 2. instead of 3. year after year 4. A number of
B-2 1. was in use 2. was involved with 3. came close to 4. died out
C   related, extinct, official, restored, replaced, bearing, interpret, comprehension

UNIT 6

A-1	1. refute 2. conscious 3. prankster 4. celebrity 5. modest
A-2	1. b 2. a 3. d 4. c 5. a
A-3	1. outrageous 2. fame 3. tension 4. pursue 5. hysterics
B-1	1. for a long time 2. a bit of 3. in the end 4. on the other hand
B-2	1. make a decision 2. put an end to 3. pay for 4. seek out
C	interest, profitable, humiliation, negative, specializes, critics, reveal, privacy

UNIT 7

A-1	1. hue 2. physiological 3. potential 4. threat 5. indicator
A-2	1. d 2. c 3. b 4. d 5. a
A-3	1. adapted 2. extreme 3. shift 4. signal 5. camouflage
B-1	1. as long as 2. in search of 3. at once 4. In addition to
B-2	1. was capable of 2. came across 3. blend in with 4. is blessed with
C	change, distinguishes, mobile, surroundings, intelligent, eating, recall, abstract

UNIT 8

A-1	1. widespread 2. unprofitable 3. dismantle 4. fulfill 5. reverse
A-2	1. b 2. d 3. d 4. b 5. c
A-3	1. high-tech 2. smooth 3. route 4. orbit 5. conspiracy
B-1	1. Fortunately 2. up and down 3. from, to 4. Both, and
B-2	1. set up 2. bring back 3. is attached to 4. shut down
C	electric, transportation, profits, recognized, cable, attached, travel, economical

UNIT 9

A-1	1. gender 2. strive 3. barrier 4. republic 5. elect
A-2	1. d 2. b 3. a 4. c 5. d
A-3	1. progress 2. controversial 3. appoint 4. unprecedented 5. unity
B-1	1. to a certain point 2. To date 3. What's more 4. under surveillance
B-2	1. rose above 2. focus on 3. taught herself 4. fight against
C	first, education, leader, such as, political, positions, assassinated, achievements

UNIT 10

A-1	1. quirk 2. recount 3. sequel 4. direct 5. release
A-2	1. c 2. b 3. d 4. d 5. a
A-3	1. separate 2. notable 3. overcome 4. courteous 5. shortage
B-1	1. in search of 2. in short supply 3. how to 4. As a result of
B-2	1. set out 2. was translated into 3. make an attempt 4. Are, aware of
C	release, sequel, published, shortage, literature, knights, journey, role model

UNIT 11

A-1 1. perilous 2. establish 3. perpetuate 4. heritage 5. policy
A-2 1. d 2. b 3. a 4. c 5. b
A-3 1. harsh 2. rickety 3. tedious 4. flock 5. arrival
B-1 1. First of all 2. for the entire day 3. a multitude of 4. such as
B-2 1. specializes in 2. object to 3. setting up 4. go through
C   repression, immigration, refugees, shores, geographically, settle, traditions, commonplace

UNIT 12

A-1 1. visible 2. somewhat 3. reveal 4. goggles 5. outline
A-2 1. b 2. d 3. c 4. b 5. b
A-3 1. reflects 2. tissue 3. debate 4. principles 5. confirm
B-1 1. Whether or not 2. Even though 3. rather than 4. As a matter of fact
B-2 1. were fascinated with 2. referring to 3. take place 4. benefit from
C   thanks to, reflecting, depending on, inspired, beyond, conducted, existence, solid

UNIT 13

A-1 1. abandoned 2. occupy 3. enormous 4. tenant 5. construction
A-2 1. c 2. a 3. d 4. c 5. b
A-3 1. afford 2. convenient 3. complete 4. distinctive 5. vacant
B-1 1. on a first-come-first-service basis 2. in that 3. at the beginning 4. far from
B-2 1. is meant to 2. planning on 3. give[giving] out 4. turned out
C   once again, tenants, intended, icon, renowned, occupied, views, connects

UNIT 14

A-1 1. admiration 2. severe 3. majority 4. previous 5. disagreement
A-2 1. d 2. c 3. b 4. d 5. c
A-3 1. process 2. search party 3. reincarnation 4. remote 5. hut
B-1 1. just as 2. Due to 3. According to 4. To this day
B-2 1. was involved in 2. date back to 3. passed away 4. narrowed down
C   religious, commences, reincarnation, continuing, dating back, meeting, voting, permitted

UNIT 15

A-1 1. sibling 2. slender 3. receive 4. legendary 5. the suburbs
A-2 1. d 2. a 3. c 4. a 5. b
A-3 1. comfort 2. daring 3. extensive 4. secondhand 5. impressed
B-1 1. all over the world 2. Not long after 3. in order to 4. right away
B-2 1. Are, familiar with 2. was responsible for 3. looking for 4. is, known as
C   influence, formal, apprenticed, provocative, poverty, orphanage, connections, comfortable

UNIT 16

A-1   1. significant   2. comprise   3. engage   4. commercial   5. sponsor

A-2   1. c   2. c   3. d   4. b   5. d

A-3   1. current   2. deplete   3. justify   4. alleged   5. moratorium

B-1   1. in the name of   2. all the way   3. in response to   4. Over time

B-2   1. making the headlines   2. resulted in   3. was dedicated to   4. engages in

C   crew, block, controversy, unlawful, floating, current, trapped in, launched

memo

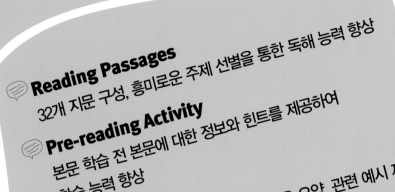

Reading Passages
32개 지문 구성, 흥미로운 주제 선별을 통한 독해 능력 향상

Pre-reading Activity
본문 학습 전 본문에 대한 정보와 힌트를 제공하여
학습 능력 향상

Reading Tips
본문에서 언급한 주요 표현이나 상황을 요약, 관련 예시 제공

Comprehension Questions
내신, 수능, TOEFL을 포함한 다양한 문제 유형으로 구성

Unit Review
각 Unit별 테스트를 통해 앞에서 배운 어휘, 문법,
주요 표현 이해 및 점검

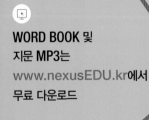

WORD BOOK 및
지문 MP3는
www.nexusEDU.kr에서
무료 다운로드